SHEILA FITZPATRICK is a leading authority on the history of the Soviet Union. She regularly contributes to the *London Review of Books*, and is the multi-award winning author of many books, including *The Shortest History of the Soviet Union*, *On Stalin's Team*, *Everyday Stalinism* and *The Russian Revolution*

GW00632266

The Death
of Stalin

GREAT  EVENTS

Sheila Fitzpatrick

UNCORRECTED PROOF COPY.

Dedication tk

Published in Great Britain in 2025 by
Old Street Publishing Ltd
Notaries House, Exeter EX1 1AJ

www.oldstreetpublishing.co.uk

ISBN 978-1-91308-393-9
Ebook ISBN 978-1-91308-370-0

10 9 8 7 6 5 4 3 2 1

A CIP catalogue record for this title is available from
the British Library.

Printed and bound in Great Britain.

TABLE OF CONTENTS

A DEATH OF STALIN TIMELINE

Note that until 1918 the "old-style" Russian calendar was 13 days behind the Western calendar.

21 December 1879	Official birthday of Stalin (actual date of birth 6 December [old-style], 1878)
August 1903	Formation of Bolshevik faction (splinter group of Russian Social-Democratic Labour Party led by Lenin), later known as the Russian, then Soviet, Communist Party (Bolsheviks)
November 1903	Stalin exile in Siberia (escapes after a couple of months)
1905–6	Revolution in Russia ('1905 Revolution'), came close to toppling Tsarist government
December 1905	Stalin's meeting with Lenin in Finland
Sept. 1910–June 1911	Stalin's second exile in Siberia
1912	Stalin co-opted to Bolshevik Central Committee
June 1913–Feb 1917	Stalin's third exile in Siberia
March 1917	'February [old style calendar] Revolution,' abdication of Emperor Nicholas II
November 1917	'October [old style calendar] Revolution" Bolsheviks take power
1918–20	Civil War in Russia between 'Reds' and 'Whites'
16 March 1921	Factions banned in resolution of Tenth Party Congress 'On Party Unity'
3 April 1922	Stalin appointed General Secretary of the Communist (Bolshevik) Party
26 May 1922	Lenin's first stroke
21 January 1924	Lenin's death
31 January 1924	Formal establishment of the Soviet Union
January 1924	Victory of 'Central Committee majority' (including Stalin) over Trotsky-led ('Left Opposition')
Oct–Nov 1927	Defeat of 'United Opposition'; Trotsky sent into internal exile
11 February 1929	Trotsky's deportation from Soviet Union
1928	Collectivization drive begins
1929-32	First Five-Year Plan
21 December 1929	Stalin's 50th birthday celebrated

November 1929	Defeat of 'Right Opposition'
5 December 1936	Stalin Constitution
(l. 1936 to l. 1938)	Great Purges
23 August 1939	German-Soviet Non-Aggression Pact signed
22 June 1941	German attack on the Soviet Union
June 1941–May 1945	'Great Patriotic War' (Second World War)
July 1942–Feb. 1943	Battle of Stalingrad
6 August 1945	Atomic bomb dropped by US on Hiroshima
25 March 1946	Churchill's 'Iron curtain' speech in Fulton, Missouri
3 April 1948	Marshall Plan (Economic Recovery Act) signed by US President Truman
24 June 1948– 12 May 1949	Berlin crisis (Soviets impose blockade, Allies airlift supplies)
21 December 1949	Stalin's 70th birthday celebrated
25 June 1950	Outbreak of Korean war
13 January 1953	Arrest of Kremlin doctors announced
20 January 1953	Inauguration of US President Harry S. Truman
1 March 1953	Stalin suffers a stroke
5 March 1953	Stalin dies
4 April 1953	Announcement of release of Kremlin doctors
26 June 1953	Beria's arrest
27 July 1953	Armistice in Korean War
23 December 1953	Beria's execution
25 February 1956	Khrushchev's 'Secret Speech' at Twentieth Party Congress
4 November 1956	Soviet invasion of Hungary
June 1957	Khrushchev's defeat of 'anti-party group'
October 1961	Twenty-Second Party Congress
31 October 1961	Moving of Stalin's body from Mausoleum to Kremlin Wall
October 1964	Khrushchev's ouster by Brezhnev
August 1968	Soviet invasion of Czechoslovakia
December 1979	Soviet invasion of Afghanistan
1986–1991	Gorbachev's perestroika
25 December 1991	Dissolution of the Soviet Union
2000	Putin becomes President of Russia

CAST OF CHARACTERS

* * *

Alliluyeva, Nadezhda Sergeevna (Nadya) (1901–1932)
Daughter of revolutionary friend of Stalin active in Caucasus before
the revolution; married Stalin as second wife in 1918, mother of
Svetlana and Vasily. Engineering student at Industrial Academy.
Shot herself after quarrel with Stalin at party, 7 November 1932.

Alliluyeva, Svetlana (1926–2011)
Daughter of Joseph Stalin and his second wife Nadezhda Alliluyeva, married to Grigory Morozov (1944–7) and Yuri Zhdanov
(1949–52), defected to US 1967.

Andreyeva, Nina Alexandrovna (1938–2020)
Chemistry teacher, joined party 1966, critical of perestroika, published essay 'I cannot forsake my principles' 13 March 1988.

**Beria, Lavrenty Pavlovich
(1899–1953)**
Georgian, joined Bolsheviks March
1917, leaded Georgian secret police
1926–31, then 1st secretary of Georgian
(Transcaucasian) party in 1930s, to
Moscow 1938 as national head of the
secret police, candidate member of
Politburo 1939, full member 1946.
Most active reformer in post–Stalin
'collective leadership' until arrest by
colleagues June 1953 and execution
December 1953.

Brezhnev, Leonid Ilyich (1906–1982)
Born Ukraine, identified as Russian, joined Komsomol 1923 then
party 1929. Promoted to regional leadership Dnepropetrovsk in
wake of Great Purges; political commissar in Army during World
War II, 1st secretary Dnepropetrosk after war (working with
Khrushchev, his later patron); full member of Politburo 1957,

supporting Khrushchev against Anti-Party group; 1964 spearheaded removal of Khrushchev; de facto leader of Politburo and Soviet Union until his death.

Bukharin, Nikolai Ivanovich (1888–1938)

Russian, joined Bolsheviks as student in 1906, then in emigration, Politburo member from 1924–9, ousted as 'Right Oppositionist 1929, defendant in show trial 1938, shot as 'enemy of the people.'

Bulganin, Nikolai Alexandrovich (1895–1975)

Russian, joined Bolsheviks 1917, deputy minister for defence under Stalin 1944, then minister 1947–55; full member of Politburo 1948–58.

Churchill, Sir Winston (1974–1965)

British statesman, organizer of British intervention on side of Whites in Russian Civil War, 1919–21; anti-appeasement of Nazi Germany late 1930s, then Prime Minister 1940–45 (establishing good personal relations with Stalin) and 1951–55. Delivered 'Iron curtain' speech in Fulton, Missouri, 5 March 1946, but after Stalin's death critical of US Secretary of State John Foster Dulles and pushed unsuccessfully for a Summit meeting with Soviet Union.

Djilas, Milovan (1911–1995)

Yugoslav communist, wartime partisan working with Josip Broz Tito, visited Moscow and met Stalin 1944 and 1948, minister in Tito's postwar government until 1953, subsequently in political disgrace after supporting 1956 Hungarian uprising.

Dobrynin, Anatoly Fedorovich (1919–2010)

Soviet diplomat, Ambassador in Washington 1962–86, associated with détente.

Dudintsev, Vladimir Dmitrievich (1918–1998)
Soviet writer, author of a Thaw hit, *Not By Bread Alone* (1956) and perestroika follow-up *White Robes* (1987).

Dulles, Allen W. (1893–1969)
Office of Strategic Services during Second World War, deputy director, then director of CIA 1951–1961. Brother of John Foster Dulles.

Dulles, John Foster (1888–1959)
Republican US Senator 1949, US Secretary of State 1953–9, hard-liner on Soviet Union. Brother of Allen Dulles.

Ehrenburg, Ilya Grigorevich (1891–1967)
Soviet writer and journalist, Jewish, well-connected in Soviet political circles, foreign correspondent Spanish Civil War and Second World War, author of *The Thaw* (1954) and influential reform-oriented memoirs published in the 1960s.

Ezhov, Nikolai Ivanovich (1895–1940)
Joined party 1917, working-class origin, worked in Central Committee apparat before becoming head of secret police 1936 and presiding over Great Purges; shot.

Iannucci, Armando (1963–)
British satirist, creator of TV series on British and US politics (*The Thick of It; Veep*); director of film *The Death of Stalin* (2017), acclaimed in West but banned in Russia, based on graphic novel by Fabien Nury, *La mort de Staline*.

Kaganovich, Lazar Moiseevich (1893–1991)
Jewish working-class, joined Bolsheviks 1911, 1st secretary Moscow party in 1930s, then in charge of railways and various industries; Politburo member 1930–57, ousted as member of 'Anti-Party Group' 1957.

Kamenev, Lev Borisovich (born Rozenfeld, 1883–1936)
Jewish intellectual, joined Marxist revolutionaries in 1901 and Bolsheviks in 1903, Politburo member 1919–25, with Zinoviev leader of Left Opposition, expelled from party December 1927, defendant in Moscow show trial 1936, shot.

Khrushchev, Nikita Sergeevich (1894–1971)

Russian, born Ukraine, joined party 1918, succeeded Kaganovich as 1st secretary of Moscow party organization 1935, head of Ukrainian party 1938–49, full member of Politburo (then called Presidium) from 1938, launched de-Stalinization campaign with Secret Speech at Twentieth Party Congress 1956, ousted 1964.

Kirov, Sergei Mironovich (1886–1934)

Russian, joined Bolsheviks 1904, worked Caucasus in Civil War, head of Leningrad party committee 1926–34, friend of Stalin, Full member of Politburo 1930, assassinated 1934.

Istomina, Valentina Vasilevna (1915–1994)

Housekeeper at Stalin's dacha.

Lazurkina, Dora Abramovna (born Klebanova, 1884–1974)

Marxist revolutionary from 1902, Bolshevik underground worker, after revolution held senior positions in education and party control, arrested in Great Purges 1937, released from Gulag and rehabilitated 1955.

Lenin, Vladimir Ilyich (real name Ulyanov) (1870–1924)

Russian, in Russian revolutionary movement since youth, founder in 1903 and leader of Bolshevik party (initially a faction of the Russian Social-Democratic Labour Party), in emigration in Europe 1900–05 and 1908–17, head of government and leader of party after October Revolution, sidelined by strokes from 1922.

Lozovsky, Solomon Abramovich (born Dridzo, 1878–1952)

Jewish revolutionary, joined Bolsheviks 1905, émigré in Europe 1908–17, head of Soviet propaganda agency Sovinformbiuro during war with supervisory responsibility for Jewish Anti-Fascist Committee (JAC), defendant in trial of JAC 1952, shot.

Malenkov, Georgy Maximilianovich (1901-1988)
Russian, joined party as engineering student, worked Central Committee office in mid 1920s, in charge of party organizations and then personnel department in 1930s, full member of Politburo 1946-57, head of Soviet government 1953-5, ousted as member of 'Anti-party group' 1957.

Mao Tse Tung (Zedong) (1893-1976)
Chinese Communist revolutionary, foundation leader of People's Republic of China 1949 initiator of China's 'Great Leap Forward' in late 1950s. Relations with Stalin sometimes rocky but critical of Khrushchev's de-stalinization in 1956.

Mikoyan, Anastas Ivanovich (1895-1978)
Armenian, Bolshevik from 1915, full member of Politburo 1935-66, main governmental responsibilities in external and internal trade and supply. Supporter of Khrushchev and de-stalinization in mid- 1950s; headed Rehabilitation Commission for purge victims.

Mlynář, Zdeněk (1930-1997)
Czech communist, studied law Moscow State University in early 1950s and friend of fellow-student Mikhail Gorbachev, active in Prague Spring (1968) and subsequently expelled from Party after Soviet invasion, emigrated as dissident 1977.

Molotov, Vyacheslav Mikhailovich (born Skryabin, 1890-1986)
Russian, joined Bolsheviks as student 1906, full member of Politburo 1924-57, headed Soviet government 1930-41, foreign minister 1939-49 and 1953-6, negotiated German-Soviet Non-Aggression

Pact 1939. In disgrace, but still holding senior positions, 1949 to Stalin's death. See also Zhemchuzhina, Polina (wife).

Nury, Fabien (1976-)
French cartoonist and scriptwriter; author, with artist Thierry Robin, of graphic novel *La mort de Staline* (2010) on which Iannucci's film *The Death of Stalin* is based.

Ordzhonikidze, Grigory Konstantinovich ('Sergo,' 1886-1937)
Georgian, joined Bolshevik 1904, Bolshevik Central Committee member from 1912, headed heavy industry during first two Five-year Plans, full member of Politburo 1930-37. Close friend of Stalin's until they fell out in lead-up to Great Purges late 1936, committed suicide early 1937.

Pospelov, Petr Nikolaevich (1898-1979)
Joined Bolsheviks as student 1816, worked in Central Committee office in 1920s, one of principal authors, under Stalin's supervision, of *The History of the Communist Party of the Soviet Union (Bolsheviks): Short Course* (1938); Central Committee secretary and Khrushchev ally 1953-1960.

Prokofiev, Sergei Sergeevich (1891-1953)
Renowned Russian/Soviet composer, in emigration after revolution but returned to Soviet Union in 1936 with wife Lina (separated 1941; divorced 1947), criticized by Zhdanov with other 'modernists' in late 1940s, died 5 March 1953, same day as Stalin.

Prokofieva, Lina (born Carolina Codina, 1897-1989)
Spanish singer, first wife (married 1923) of composer Sergei Prokofiev; separated from him 1941; divorced 1947; arrested 20 February 1948; freed from Gulag 1956; left the Soviet Union 1974.

Putin, Vladimir Vladimirovich (1952–)

Leningrad working-class origins, economics graduate, then KGB intelligence officer, in Dresden (East Germany) 1985-1990; after collapse of Soviet Union 1991, government work in St. Petersburg under Anatoly Sobchak, then to Moscow as deputy chief of President Yeltsin's staff; president of Russian Federation 2000-08 and 2012 to present (Prime Minister 2008-12).

Roosevelt, Franklin D. (1882–1945)

President of United States 1933-45, Democrat, initiator of 'New Deal' in 1930s; worked closely with Stalin during the Second World War, his death on 12 April 1945 much regretted in Soviet Union.

Sinyavsky, Andrei Donatovich (1925–1967)

Russian/Soviet literary critic and writer, worked in literary institute with Svetlana Stalina in 1950s, published *The Trial Begins* (1960) abroad under pseudonym, tried and convicted of 'anti-Soviet propaganda' 1966; released from Gulag 1971, emigrated to France 1973.

Shostakovich, Dmitri Dmitrevich (1906–1975)

Renowned composer, celebrity in Soviet Union from early successes in 1930s, despite being subject of official censure for modernism in 1936 and 1948; lauded in West and within Soviet intelligentsia as quasi-dissident but joined Communist Party 1960.

Solzhenitsyn, Alexander Isaevich (1918–2008)

Arrested while serving World War II and Soviet Army officer, in Gulag 1945-53, made career as writer, initially under *Novy mir* sponsorship, with Gulag novel *One Life in the Life of Ivan Denisovich* (1962), followed by *First Circle* (1968) and the non-fictional *Gulag Archipelago,* (1974). Expelled from Soviet Union 1974; returned to Russia 1994.

Stalin, Iosif Vissarionovich (born Dzugashvili, 1878–1953)

Georgian, in Marxist revolutionary movement from 1898, Bolshevik from 1903. Founding member of Politburo, which he led from the mid 1920s until his death, general secretary of the party from 1922. Married (1) Ekaterina Svanidze, and 2) Nadezhda Alliluyeva (see separate entry); children Yakov (1907–43), Vasily (see separate entry) and Svetlana (see separate entry)

Stalina, Svetlana Iosifovna: see Alliluyeva, Stalina

Stalin, Vasily Iosifovich (1921–1962)

Son of Stalin and Nadezhda Alliluyeva, in air-force during and after Second World War, reaching rank of Lieut.-General; heavy drinker, imprisoned for anti-Soviet behavior April 1953–60, then retired on pension.

Trotsky, Lev Davidovich (born Bronshtein, 1879–1940)

Joined Marxist revolutionary movement 1897, Menshevik until mid 1917, when he joined the Bolsheviks; prominent in 1905 and 1917 Revolutions in St. Petersburg/Petrograd, leader of Red Army in Civil War, leader of 'Left Opposition' after Lenin's death; expelled from party 1927 and sent into internal exile; deported from USSR to Turkey 1929, assassinated in Mexico by Soviet agents.

Truman, Harry S. (1884–1972)

Vice-President of US under President Roosevelt, succeeding on Roosevelt's death mid term; President April 1945–January 1953; Democrat but viewed by Soviets as hostile, failing to establish rapport with Stalin at Potsdam Conference (August 1945), presiding over onset of Cold War with Berlin airlift and Marshall Plan (1948).

Tvardovsky, Alexander Trifonovich (1910–1971)

Soviet poet, son of peasant exiled as 'kulak' in early 1930s, author of popular wartime epic *Vasily Terkin*, reform-minded editor of journal *Novy mir* (1950-4 and 1958-70), publishing Solzhenitsyn, Ehrenburg and Yevtushenko in 1960s.

Walter Ulbricht (1893-1973)
German Communist politician, head Socialist Unity [Communist] Party 1950-71, one of founders of German Democratic Republic (GDR) in 1949, head of its government.

Vinogradov, Dr. Vladimir Nikitich (1882-1964)
Distinguished Soviet medical expert, member Academy of Medical Sciences 1944. Personal physician to Stalin and other Politburo members, one of the accused in 'Doctors' Plot,' announced January 1953; released after a few months and resumed medical career.

Vlasik, Nikolai Sidorich (1896-1967)
Worked in Soviet security organs, from early 1930s on Stalin's personal security team, becoming close to family after death of Stalin's wife. Removed from position 15 December 1952, convicted on corruption charges. Pardoned 1956.

Voroshilov, Kliment Efremovich (1881-1969)
Russian, born Ukraine in family of railway worker, joined Bolsheviks 1903; fought with cavalry in Civil War (working with Stalin at Tsaritsyn, later Stalingrad); minister of defence 1925-40; full member of Politburo 1925-60.

Voznesensky, Nikolai Alekseevich (1903-1950)
Russian, joined party 1919, worked in planning commission in Leningrad and Moscow, full member of Politburo 1947, removed from all posts March 1949, then arrested and shot.

Yevtushenko, Yevgeny Aleksandrovich (1933-2017)
Russian/Soviet poet and writer, Siberian born, came to prominence in Thaw with poems on *Babi Yar* (1961) and *Heirs of Stalin* (1962); but political standing dimmed after he signed protest against Soviet invasion of Czechoslovakia in 1968. During perestroika, directed little-known film *Stalin's Funeral* (1990) starring Vanessa Redgrave as one of two lovers who meet in the funeral crowd.

Zhdanov, Andrei Aleksandrovich (1896–1948)

Russian, joined party as student 1915, party secretary in Nizhny Novgorod (later Gorky) 1922–34 and Leningrad 1934–44; full member of Politburo 1939–48; headed 'anti-cosmopolitan' campaign after the war.

Zhdanov, Yuri Andreevich (1919–2006)

Son of Andrei, chemist, headed Science Department of party Central Committee 1948–53' married to Svetlana Stalina 1949–52.

Zhemchuzhina, Polina Semenovna (born Karpovskaya, 1897–1970)

Jewish tailor's daughter, joined party 1918; political commissar with Red Army in Civil War, married Molotov 1920; senior posts in cosmetic industry in 1930s and light industry 1939–48; arrested as Zionist 1949 (Molotov had to divorce her), returned from exile and resumed life with Molotov March 1953.

Zhukov, Georgy Konstantinovich (1896–1974)

Russian, professional military in Red Army from 1918, joined party 1919, army general 1940, marshal 1943, deputy to Stalin as Supreme Commander of military in Second World War, led victory parade Moscow 1945, demoted 1946, minister of defence 1955–7, key ally of Khrushchev in arrest of Beria and ouster of Anti-Party group.

Zinoviev, Grigory Evseevich (born Radomylsky, 1883–1936)

Jewish, in Marxist revolutionary movement from 1901, Bolshevik 1903, émigré close to Lenin before 1917. After revolution, headed Leningrad party organization until 1926, Politburo member 1921–6, in alliance with Stalin against Trotsky in succession struggle after Lenin's death but then joined Trotsky in opposition; defendant in 1936 Moscow show trial, shot.

INTRODUCTION

By the early 1950s, Joseph Stalin had been unchallenged leader of the Soviet Union for over twenty years, having presided over a ruthless economic modernization drive in the early 1930s, a bout of terror known as the Great Purges in the late 1930s, the near catastrophe and ultimate victory of World War II, and the Soviet Union's emergence as a superpower in the postwar world. There had only been one other leader since the Russian Revolution of October 1917 had laid the foundation of the new state: Vladimir Lenin, the Bolshevik (Communist) Party's founder, who had died only seven years later. Stalin was surrounded by an officially-inspired cult that made him seem godlike; no clear successor was in sight. After almost thirty years, his death in 1953 was bound to be a deeply unsettling event in the Soviet Union.

It was a bipolar world, thanks to the Cold War, with two superpowers, the United States and the Soviet Union, locked in hostile confrontation. The US feared that the Soviet aim was to conquer the world for communism; the Soviet Union considered the US an aggressive power bent on extending the reach of the 'free world'. The Soviet Union, like the United States, had acquired nuclear weapons capable of inflicting enormous destruction. Each side feared a first pre-emptive strike by the other.

The wartime alliance was in tatters, having given way to demonization on both sides. Stalin frequently stated his commitment to peace; and contemporary scholarship basically accepts that indeed he thought his war-damaged country too weak to fight another war in the short term. To Western contemporaries, however, it looked different. The Soviet Union, leader of the world communist movement, appeared as an aggressive, expansionist power with an ideology inimical to the West, capable of igniting a Third World War. Fears of imminent conflagration grew with the Berlin crisis of 1948 and the outbreak of the Korean war (then understood as a Soviet initiative) a few years later.

1

With Soviet high politics a black box both to the Soviet public and the West, Stalin's death in March 1953 threatened to plunge both the Soviet Union and the world into turmoil. In his *The Death of Stalin*, the British film director Armando Iannucci memorably depicted the death scene as black comedy, with Stalin's potential successors united only by ambition and relief, milling around distractedly at his deathbed. That is indeed how the main eye-witness accounts describe it, although to be sure these were eye-witnesses with their own agendas. There is black comedy in this book too, not just in connection with Stalin's death but also with the fate of his corporeal remains (buried, dug up, reburied) and the subsequent persistent apparitions of his ghost. But not everything about Stalin's death is comic. It had serious implications for his country and the world in the twentieth century and beyond; this book sets out to unravel them.

CHAPTER 1

Stalin

Stalin in the
early 1900s

Joseph Vissarionovich Dzhugashvili did not look destined for
greatness at his birth in 1879. He was the son of a drunken
cobbler and an ambitious mother in the small town of Gori in
Georgia, a distant southern province of the Russian Empire,
acquired through imperial conquest at the beginning of the
nineteenth century. What was unusual about Dzhugashvili
was not only that he transcended lowly origins to rise to greatness but also that he achieved this via the usually dead-end
route of being a revolutionary.

Thanks to his mother's efforts, the young Dzhugashvili
had received the best education available for someone of his
origins at the Orthodox Seminary in the capital, Tiflis (now
Tbilisi). But like many other seminarians of his generation,
he soon abandoned Christianity and embraced an alternative belief system, revolution. There were various forms
of revolutionary affiliation available, all involving illegal

3

underground activity. Georgian nationalist or socialist were the two chief options, with the socialist revolutionaries in Georgia mainly Marxist, which meant a commitment both to the urban working class (the 'proletariat', in Marxist terms) and to internationalism. Early on, Dzhugashvili was tempted by nationalism, and even wrote some romantic poetry in the Georgian language before switching onto the internationalist Marxist revolutionary track. The place he found for himself in the revolutionary movement in Georgia was militant and often non-collegial. He liked to be called Koba, after a Robin Hood-like bandit of Georgian folk lore.

Georgia was the boondocks as far as revolution in the Russian empire was concerned. Dzhugashvili aimed to participate at a higher level, namely in Russia, and the Tsarist police facilitated this aspiration by sending him into exile in the cold Siberian north, where he served three separate terms, a short one at the end of 1903 and two longer ones totalling almost five years in the 1910s. The Russian Marxists had split in the early years of the century into Bolsheviks, the tougher, maximalist group led by Vladimir Ulyanov, who went by the revolutionary name Lenin, and the more moderate and numerous Mensheviks. Dzhugashvili aligned himself with the Bolsheviks, both because of his admiration for Lenin and his dislike for the Mensheviks who led the Marxist revolutionary movement in Georgia.

It was a time of hope for Russian revolutionaries. In 1905, a year-long upheaval sparked by Russia's defeat in war with Japan almost toppled the Tsar. Although the old regime hung on, it was with damaged credibility. Nevertheless, most of the revolutionary leaders, including Lenin and his Menshevik competitor Lev Trotsky, were driven into exile. Dzhugashvili was one of the Russia-based revolutionaries who made arduous journeys to Europe to attend the party's conferences, starting in December 1905. Lenin, who was always keen to add names to his (illegal) mailing list and hear first-hand news of the situation in Russia, welcomed this 'marvellous Georgian' (although temporarily forgetting his name) and Dzhugashvili returned home impressed. He never took to the revolutionary café society of 'abroad', however, and considered its habitués

4

(except for Lenin) dilettantes. There was a class element to this too. Most of the revolutionary émigrés were university drop-outs from noble or intelligentsia families who could afford to support their errant sons in Europe. Those like Dzhugashvili who stuck to illegal work at home, with the attendant stints of prison and internal exile, tended to be of lower social class and less formal education.

Dzhugashvili started writing under the name Stalin – a Russian-sounding coinage meaning 'man of steel', probably modelled on Ulyanov's *nom de guerre*, Lenin – in the 1910s, and ultimately adopted it as his name, dropping the clearly Georgian Dzhugashvili. But if Dzhugashvili was assuming a Russian identity, it had nothing to do with what he would have called 'bourgeois' Russian nationalism. True, there was a positive attraction to things Russian: Dzhugashvili/Stalin always fondly remembered the hunting and fishing friends he made in exile in Siberia, and he would later develop great respect for, and considerable knowledge of, Russian high culture. At the time, however, becoming Stalin meant ceasing to be a provincial in the Russian revolutionary movement and graduating to the status of an 'all-Russian' revolutionary rather than just a Georgian one. Dzhugashvili's education in Gori and Tiflis had been in Russian, and he spoke it fluently, if with a strong Georgian accent. He never resided in Georgia again after his young wife's death from typhus and a 1907 scandal over his involvement in 'expropriations' (robbing banks for the revolution, a step too far for Marxist revolutionary purists). His identity change was as much about repudiating (or rising above) Georgianness as it was about as embracing Russianness. Indeed, like other internationally-minded revolutionaries and progressives, he was studying Esperanto at the same time.

Man of steel

Lenin's revolution
Stalin, a member of the Bolshevik Central Committee since 1912, was one of the first Bolsheviks to make it back to Petrograd (formerly and now St Petersburg, later Leningrad) after the February Revolution of 1917. This was because he happened to be closer to the scene than Lenin and other

émigré revolutionaries, stuck in Europe on the wrong side of the front in the First World War, in which Russia, fighting on the side of the Allies against Germany, had suffered a string of humiliating military defeats. The mood among revolutionaries was euphoric. For once, they were prepared to put aside their normal factional struggles, the better to represent the socialist cause in the power-sharing arrangement that had emerged since February between the socialists dominating the soviets (ad hoc councils established spontaneously by workers and soldiers) and the liberals dominating the Provisional Government. Stalin and other Bolsheviks on site went along with the unity consensus – that is, until Lenin finally made it back from Switzerland in April and dramatically took an intransigent stand. 'All power to the soviets' was Lenin's slogan, meaning forget about unity, think about further revolution to overthrow the Provisional Government. Actually Lenin was not much interested in soviets, and neither was Stalin. They were the provenance of the charismatic Trotsky, a former Menshevik who joined Lenin and the Bolsheviks only in mid 1917. It was with Trotsky's indispensable help that the Bolshevik party took power in the name of the soviets in October.

Bolsheviks take power

In power, Lenin was no more interested in cooperating with other revolutionaries than he had been out of it. The Bolsheviks set up a government, headed by Lenin, but the real locus of power was in the party's Politburo, in which Lenin held no formal leadership position but was the acknowledged first among equals. As Marxists, the Bolsheviks conceptualized the revolution as a proletarian one, historically determined, since capitalism was bound at some time to be overthrown by the workers it exploited. In the long run, theoretically, the state would wither away and the population self-organize in local soviets. In the short run, however, a 'dictatorship of the proletariat' was needed to consolidate the revolution and defeat its enemies. These included the 'Whites', who took up arms and fought the Bolshevik 'Reds' in a three-year Civil War, and also 'class enemies' such as landowners, rich peasants, clergy and nobility who were assumed, regardless of their individual actions or stated political views, to be hostile to the revolution. The Bolshevik Party, as a self-declared 'vanguard of the proletariat', was the real-life instrument of proletarian dictatorship. Other parties were successively outlawed.

If Lenin held to a hard line on politics, he was more flexible when it came to economics. During the Civil War, the Bolsheviks had tried to establish basic institutions of state socialism such as nationalized trade, industry and financial institutions ('War communism'). In 1921, in face of economic near-collapse, Lenin had pushed through the New Economic Policy (NEP), partially re-establishing market relations and making various conciliatory moves towards the peasantry and the 'bourgeois' intelligentsia (relabelled as 'specialists' whose expertise was needed by the revolution). These concessions worked, but they went against the grain of many party activists.

Stalin was a member of the Politburo since its inception in August 1917, But in these first years, he was not one of the glamorous Bolsheviks, such as Lenin, Trotsky or Grigory Zinoviev, who had returned with Lenin from Switzerland to become the party's top man in Petrograd. Younger than Lenin and the other party intellectuals, he was also unlike them in being a self-educated provincial who spoke Russian with an accent. Foreigners – diplomats, newspaper correspondents, spies – were on calling terms with Trotsky and, less often, with Lenin, but rarely if ever with Stalin. After a not particularly distinguished stint as a political commissar at the front in the Civil War, Stalin became the quintessential backroom man, a function formalized with his appointment as general secretary of the party in April 1922.

Becomes general secretary

In these years, Stalin was usually seen as a mere executant for Lenin. But he and Lenin did sometimes disagree in the only area in which Stalin claimed special expertise, nationalities policy. In 1920, Stalin cautioned against the military attack on Poland that Lenin hoped would encourage workers' revolution in that country. Stalin's view was that, in the face of what would be interpreted as a Russian attack, Polish workers would support the Polish government (as indeed proved to be the case). He had, however, taken a different stand the previous year, when he approved the Red Army's invasion of Georgia, at that point under control of the Georgian Mensheviks Stalin had disliked for decades.

The Bolsheviks had taken power in a multinational empire that was in the process of crumbling. They were internationalists, expecting world revolution to follow their own revolution in Russia (the weakest link in the capitalist chain, according to Trotsky). They were in no sense Russian nationalists, and had no a priori commitment to keeping the territory of the former Russian empire together as a political unit. But it was on the territory of the old Russian empire that the Red Army fought a civil war with the Whites, and this imposed its own logic. Of course the Bolsheviks wanted revolution to succeed in the non-Russian parts of the old empire, just as in its Russian ones – and, for that matter, the whole of Europe. Victory in the civil war meant that 'revolution' had triumphed in most of the old Russian empire (minus Finland, Russia's Polish provinces, and the Baltic states). There was still hope that it would go on to triumph in Europe, although by the early 1920s this was looking less likely than at the end of the First World War. In the meantime, in any case, the successful revolution in former Russian imperial territories needed to mould itself into a state.

What form should this revolutionary state take? There were no precedents, and Marxist theory was little help. The options were a multi-national federation and a union of national republics. In the course of the civil war, revolutionary Russia had declared itself to be a Russian Socialist Federal Soviet Republic (RSFSR) governed from Moscow (which had replaced Petrograd as Russia's capital in 1918). Non-Russian ethnic groups like the Buryats and the Kazan Tatars were given their own autonomous administrative units within the federation. When the question arose about how to incorporate Ukraine, Georgia, Armenia and other larger non-Russian territories, Stalin thought they too should be admitted into the RSFSR as autonomous regions. Lenin favoured giving the major non-Russian nationalities their own republics inside a larger union, with the formal power to secede as well as substantial powers over domestic matters such as education and use of the native language in administration. It was Lenin's view that prevailed; and the Union of Socialist Soviet Republics, or USSR, formally came into being on 31 January 1924.

USSR is born

The date was just ten days after Lenin's untimely death from a stroke at the age of 53. This was the last in a series of strokes, starting in May 1922, that, to Lenin's great frustration, had progressively removed him from active participation in political life. In his last years, he accused his Politburo colleagues collectively of becoming an oligarchy, and, in a document labelled retrospectively 'Lenin's Testament', surveyed their individual qualities for leadership and found them all to some degree wanting. Stalin, who as the party's general secretary had been given the thankless job of seeing that Lenin followed doctors' orders to keep out of politics, incurred Lenin's particular wrath. As a result, Lenin added a postscript to the Testament saying that Stalin's 'rudeness' made him unsuitable for his position as party secretary. This was a personal blow to Stalin, who looked up to Lenin, and potentially a major political setback in the undeclared succession struggle precipitated by Lenin's illness.

Trotsky was the apparent front-runner in this struggle, as the organizer of victory in the Civil War. Stalin had notoriously bad relations with Trotsky, who made little attempt to hide his contempt for those he saw as intellectually inferior. They had clashed repeatedly during the Civil War, when Trotsky commanded the Red Army and Stalin was a political commissar at the front. Trotsky dismissed Stalin as a nonentity – which, judging by the degree of his hostility, is perhaps how he wanted Stalin seen, rather than how he privately saw him. The tactic worked well with future historians, who like to quote Trotsky's characterization, but was less successful with party members at the time. For provincial party officials, Stalin, as national party secretary, was a familiar and approachable figure, and Trotsky an arrogant and elusive one. Trotsky, moreover, remained suspect to some Old Bolsheviks as a newcomer to the party, and, by analogy with the French Revolution, a potential 'Bonaparte', that is, a military leader in revolutionary wars, enabled by victory to become a dictator. On top of that, he was a Jew, which Trotsky himself regarded as a disqualification for leadership in Russia. Most of the other plausible leadership candidates were also Jewish, and all except Stalin were Westernized intellectuals, another potential drawback in a mainly lower-class party.

Stalin, Rykov,
Kamenev, and
Zinoviev in
1925

As Lenin had only an informal status as leader of the
Bolshevik Party (now renamed the Communist Party of the
Soviet Union, although the old label stayed in use for many
years), there was no formal position up for grabs. Still, the
election of delegates for the upcoming national party conference gave local party organizations what was in effect a vote
on succession, since Trotsky and his supporters put forward
their own policy platform and a slate of candidates, in opposition to that of their Politburo colleagues, including Stalin,
who offered the platform and candidates of 'the Central
Committee majority'. Separate policy platforms were suspect,
since in 1921 Lenin had pushed through a ban on factions,
which the Trotsky group was clearly ignoring. In 1924, the
'Central Committee majority' won. While it was not immediately clear to Zinoviev and others in the group that this
meant that Stalin was the emerging successor to Lenin, Stalin
adroitly engineered a series of splits that pushed Zinoviev and
his ally Lev Kamenev (another Jewish intellectual and former
émigré) into factional opposition as well. By 1927, when Trotsky, Zinoviev, and other 'Oppositionists' were banished from
Moscow into internal exile, Stalin's primacy was assured.

The Politburo elected at the national party congress of that
year included Stalin supporters such as Vyacheslav Molotov (a

dour Russian from the provinces who had joined the Bolsheviks as a university student in 1906), the Jewish working-class Lazar Kaganovich (party member since 1911, a political commissar during the Civil War) and the charismatic Klim Voroshilov (son of a Russian railway worker in Ukraine, one of the leaders of the Red Army in the Civil War) who would be fixtures, along with Stalin, for decades. For them, Stalin was not a nonentity but a tough, focussed, resourceful and determined person who was a natural leader. They admired his intelligence and his combination of outward calm and political boldness, and looked up to him (a decade or so older than most of them) as the wiliest political tactician and strategist of them all. 'We were greenhorns' beside him, Molotov later recalled.

Stalin's revolution

In the policy debates of the succession struggle, Stalin looked like a centrist. Trotsky and later Zinoviev were branded 'leftists', while a group ousted later that included Nikolai Bukharin was labelled 'rightist'. Accepting this narrative, Western observers generally welcomed Stalin's victory. They took it to mean that, after going off the rails with the revolution in 1917, Russia was starting to normalize. The same possibility was under discussion among Soviet Communists, too, but for them it was not a hope but a fear – that the October Revolution was entering its own 'Thermidor', a term, borrowed from the French Revolution, that connoted embourgeoisement and waning of revolutionary energy. The Soviet Communist party was not yet ready for normalization: the will to fight 'the class enemy' and overthrow 'bourgeois' institutions was still strong, especially among Civil War veterans and the young. Political power was in the party's hands, but the transformation of the economic base that, according to Marx, was necessary to remake the social and cultural superstructure and achieve socialism had yet to happen.

Normalization and its enemies

Lenin had said that the policy shift to NEP was 'serious, and for a long time'. But that comment, a warning to party comrades to stop arguing and get on board, cannot be taken as an indication of his future intentions. When Lenin would have thought the time was ripe for a new push forward is anyone's

11

guess. But within a few years of his death, a consensus was emerging in the party leadership that a new drive on the economic front was coming, with disagreement focussing on when and how. Trotsky (the 'Leftist') was the man out front on the issue. But Stalin, speaking on the eighth anniversary of the revolution, made a similar point: 'In 1917, the issue was to make the transition from the power of the bourgeoisie to the power of the proletariat. Now, the issue is to make the transition from the present economy, which cannot be called a socialist economy, to an economy which can serve as the material basis of a socialist society.' In other words, Lenin had successfully made Revolution part 1, and it was up to his successors to get Revolution part 2 on the road.

If Stalin had been able to channel future Chinese Communist leader, Mao Tse Tung, he would have labelled Revolution part 2 the Soviet Union's 'great leap forward' (he called it, The Great Break instead, 'the Great Break'; others have called it 'Stalin's Revolution'). Starting in 1928 with a drive for mass collectivization of peasant farming, its key component was a forced-pace industrialization drive favouring heavy and defence industry and guided by a national Five-Year Plan. Private trade was outlawed in the towns. 'Class enemies' like kulaks (rich peasants), clergy and the intelligentsia came under attack in a 'cultural revolution' (another foreshadowing of Mao) which featured show trials of engineers with elaborate scenarios proving that they had been in league with Western intelligence, and a lot of cultural scapegoating by self-appointed 'proletarian' vigilantes. Political tension was high, with periodic war scares about possible attack from the West used to mobilize the public behind the Plan. State borders, already strongly controlled, were closed to the movement of goods, people, and ideas. The security police formed under the name of the Cheka back in Lenin's time, now known as the OGPU, expanded its powers and activity, laying the foundation of the Gulag convict labour empire. A Lenin cult had arisen, largely spontaneously, after the leader's death. Now the party's propaganda machine started to foster a cult of Stalin as well.

The First Five-Year Plan was proclaimed to be a success, but the costs were huge. The battle over collectivization produced a famine in the country's main grain-growing regions – Ukraine, southern Russia, Kazakhstan – in the early 1930s. Millions of peasants died, and millions more moved to the cities in search of work and food rations. Having had Trotsky deported from the country in 1929 and then crushed the last of the party factions (Bukharin's 'Right Opposition'), Stalin faced no open dissent within the party. But he assumed, not without reason, that behind his back many were criticizing his tough policies that had produced a famine in the country-side and a sharply reduced standard of living in the towns.

Stalin had always been a suspicious, untrusting man, and the suicide of his second wife Nadya in 1932, which he perceived as a betrayal as well as a loss, accentuated this characteristic. But he continued the established pattern of meeting more or less daily for some hours with Politburo members to discuss the political and governmental issues of the day, working long hours himself and expecting the same from them. His relationship with many of his colleagues was one

Beria with Stalin and his daughter in 1931.

of friendship rather than mere collegiality. Even after Nadya's death, Stalin's dacha outside Moscow remained a social centre for many of the Politburo members and their families, who – along with his Russian and Georgian in-laws – constituted Stalin's main friendship group. Young Svetlana, the red-haired daughter Stalin favoured over her two brothers, grew up with the other 'Kremlin children' as her playmates and their fathers as familiar 'uncles'.

Every great leap forward is likely to be followed by at least a few steps back. So it was with Stalin's revolution, as it had been a decade earlier with Lenin's. By 1934, it was time for a 'second NEP', in other words, a new phase of relaxation. The annual party congress was hailed as 'the congress of victors'; more consumer goods were made available in the towns; and police terror was dialled down. In a catch-phrase endlessly cited, Stalin said that 'life has become better, comrades; life has become more cheerful'. But it was not all a matter of anodyne clichés. A prodigious reader of Russian and European literature, history and politics (as the private library he collected and annotated shows), Stalin oversaw the sidelining of cultural militants and the re-establishment of 'bourgeois' writers and artists attacked during the cultural revolution. He also announced that 'a son does not answer for his father' – welcome, if surprising, news to the thousands of children of 'class enemies' whose life chances had been damaged since the Revolution by the stigma of their parents' social class. This was in line with the new Soviet ('Stalin') Constitution, over whose composition Stalin actively presided, which announced the end of class warfare in the Soviet Union, as well as guaranteeing a much broader array of rights than Soviet citizens currently enjoyed. The prominent place the Constitution occupies in Stalin's (carefully curated) personal archive suggests that he was proud of it.

On the international scene, too, things were changing. In 1917, the Bolshevik seizure of power, which led to Russian withdrawal from the First World War and a separate peace with Germany, had outraged the Allies. A whole string of foreign powers – Britain, France, Poland, Japan, the United States – supported the Whites in the Civil War in an unsuccessful effort to overthrow the revolutionary regime. The Soviet Union remained essentially a pariah nation through the 1920s, with the threat of foreign intervention never absent from the leaders' and the public's mind. Stalin and his colleagues were aware of their lack of experience with the West, compared to the Lenin cohort, and the 1930s found many of them, including Stalin, diligently studying English and German with tutors. Stalin also took it on himself to coach other Politburo members in foreign affairs, as well as editing (for grammar and style as much as content) their written work. In the mid 1930s, the Soviet Union moved towards a more cooperative relationship with other European powers, based on a shared fear of Germany, where the Nazis had come to power. In the same period, the Moscow-led Communist International switched to a policy of 'Popular Front' against fascism, which meant collaboration with the socialist and radical groups they had previously abhorred.

Then abruptly Stalin changed course again, this time towards terror. Perhaps it was the murder of his Politburo colleague and close friend Sergei Kirov in December 1934 that set off the change: the killer was a lone wolf, in fact, but Stalin took him to be part of a 'counter-revolutionary' conspiracy, with Western intelligence agencies and the exiled Trotsky pulling the strings from abroad. More show trials were held in Moscow between 1936 and 1938, with former Opposition leaders (including Zinoviev, Kamenev and Bukharin), accused of treason and terrorism, pleading guilty, and receiving the death sentence. This was accompanied by wholesale arrests, followed by long sentences to Gulag, of their associates and other members of the political elite who had allegedly turned out to be 'enemies of the people'. The mass terror that followed (labelled 'the Great Purges' in the West, but remembered in the Soviet Union simply as '1937'), was directed initially against the party itself (a first in Soviet terms), and fuelled by waves of enthusiastic popular denunciation of local Communist administrators for their abuses of power. (Many ordinary people would look back on 1937 approvingly as revolutionary democracy in action.) Communist leaders in Ukraine, Central Asia and the Caucasus were accused of 'bourgeois nationalism', a move that seriously unsettled the even-handedness of Soviet nationality policy. The terror snowballed to encompass the broader population, particularly people with foreign connections, who were accused of spying.

Stalin was clearly the initiator of and eminence behind this new terror, although he kept a low public profile during the

Murder of Kirov

Moscow show trials (while, behind the scenes, sending daily instructions about their staging). The visible executant was the head of the secret police (now re-renamed NKVD), Nikolai Ezhov, previously unremarkable but now hailed as 'the sword of the Revolution'. Even Politburo members were not safe from his blade. While most survived (although without any advance guarantees), there were many victims among their ministerial associates, staff and families. Members of Stalin's personal family circle, which consisted mainly of his two wives' Georgian and Russian relatives, also fell victim, leaving him an isolated and lonely man. They had been denounced, of course, like countless other elite members; and presumably Ezhov, out of prudence, included these denunciations in the security materials he regularly laid before Stalin. It may seem strange that Stalin did not simply tell Ezhov to ignore denunciations of his in-laws, but probably from Stalin's standpoint something like revolutionary honour was at stake (as it would be during the Second World War, when he refused to do a deal with the Germans to save his eldest son when he was taken prisoner of war). Stalin had moral authority to lose in dealing with his Politburo: if, for the duration of the Purges, their usual license to intervene with the secret police to save family and clients had been suspended, so must Stalin's be.

Molotov, head of the Soviet government throughout the 1930s, later justified the terror as the pre-emptive elimination of a Fifth Column in the coming war – an objective that, on the face of it, scarcely justified destroying almost all the country's top military leaders. But it is more likely that Stalin had a grander (in his mind) purpose, as Kaganovich later suggested,

Draining the
swamp

namely draining the 'swamp' of erstwhile revolutionaries, now jaded and venal like those whose French Revolutionary counterparts had destroyed Robespierre in Thermidor. Probably he saw the terror as a bold strike against actual and potential political enemies that would both secure his power and instil fear – and so unquestioning obedience – in the party and the population. Whatever his conscious intentions, there was doubtless an element of paranoia in play as well. But Stalin was not carried away by paranoia. Surely Stalin (and to a lesser extent his Politburo) viewed the Purges as a bold initiative which, given the risks of the terror backfiring on its author, only Stalin would have dared to take. He and they must privately have taken pride in the political skills that enabled him, after two years, to close down the bloodletting without incident and emerge with his own stature not only undamaged but even enhanced. In the wind-down, Ezhov was predictably discovered to be an enemy of the people and shot, along with other senior members of the secret police. Lavrenty Beria, a Georgian party leader and client of Stalin's, was brought up from the Caucasus to pick up the pieces.

The Second World War

Stalin and Ribbentrop shake hands in the Kremlin after signing the non-aggression pact.

It was Stalin's earnest desire to stay out of the European war that was visibly on the horizon as a result of the rise and expansionist aims of Nazi Germany. What he hoped was that the Western powers (Britain and France) and Germany would fight each other, leaving the Soviet Union to sit it out. But the British appeasement of Germany in Munich in 1938 showed that this was not on the cards. Unfortunately the Western democracies had the same idea as Stalin, but in reverse: they should sit it out while Germany and the Soviet Union fought each other. Giving up on the idea of a Western alliance, Stalin startled the Soviet public and appalled the international Left by his next move: a Non-Aggression Pact that he and Molotov negotiated with Hitler and German Foreign Minister Ribbentrop in August 1939. The Pact guaranteed that neither side would attack the other. It also (in secret clauses) gave license for German occupation of western Poland, on the one hand, and, on the other, Soviet occupation of eastern Poland and the Baltic states (independent since the revolution, but previously part of the Russian empire). This was no love affair between totalitarian dictators, but rather a desperate effort on Stalin's part to buy time to rebuild the army and create a buffer zone between Germany and the Soviet Union. The strategy failed dramatically in June 1941, when Germany, breaking the Pact without notice, launched an invasion of the Soviet Union.

Non-Aggression Pact with Germany

Having gambled and lost, Stalin's first reaction was that the Politburo would throw him out. They didn't (evidently still assuming that Stalin was the best man to lead), but the balance of power between Stalin and other members shifted, as it had done in the opposite direction during the Great Purges. New members had been added at the end of the 1930s, including the highly competent but not universally loved Beria (in charge of the secret police), the self-effacing back-room man Georgy Malenkov (head of the Central Committee's personnel department), Andrei Zhdanov (head of the Leningrad party organization during the war, known in party circles as a man of culture) and Nikita Khrushchev (the down-to-earth party leader in Ukraine in 1940s). In one of the many ironies of Soviet history, the war produced the best-functioning government that the Soviet Union had ever had, led by a body that was essentially the Politburo (although under a new name) with Stalin at its head. Despite the extraordinary success of Germany's initial invasion, the Soviet regime came through four years of its 'Great Patriotic War' without any serious threat from within via elite coup or popular unrest. In the invasion, a large part of the Soviet airforce was destroyed on the ground, and the Wehrmacht advanced rapidly not just through the new-acquired buffer territories but to the very edges of Moscow and Leningrad, at the same time driving southwards towards the Baku oilfields. Stalin took over from Voroshilov as Minister for Defence after the June 1941 debacle, made himself Supreme Commander of the Soviet armed forces with the title of Generalissimo (a comic opera touch he later regretted), and, in cooperation with his generals (newly appointed to replace the Purge victims), oversaw the military effort. On the home front, Beria was in charge of security and Gulag, with other Politburo members, including Malenkov, Mikoyan (a virtuoso at organizing supply), and Khrushchev, directing the economy and the regions.

Three boys inspect photographs of Churchill and Stalin, displayed at Charing Cross underground station in 1942 as part of a Ministry of Information exhibition – 'Comrades in Arms: Pictures of the Soviet at War'.

Foreign policy was Molotov's domain, but in fact it was a double act, with Stalin – showing an unsuspected ability to charm and impress Western leaders in personal interactions – establishing a good working relationship with Allied leaders, US President Franklin Roosevelt and British Prime Minister Winston Churchill. But for all Stalin's pleas and Churchill's evasive promises, the Allies did not open a Second Front in the West to take the pressure off the Soviet Army. On the Eastern (for a long time the only) front, the Soviet Army fought on, taking large casualties. The military tide turned at the beginning of 1943, when Soviet forces under General (later Marshal) Georgy Zhukov defeated the Germans at the Volga (a long way into Russia, if you look at the map!) in the Battle of Stalingrad. It was at this point that Stalin, now 'Uncle Joe' to the American public, made his big impact on Western opinion, featuring as *Time* magazine's Man of the Year in January 1943. It took another two years for the Soviet Army to drive the German Wehrmacht back westward and across the border. As the denouement approached, Soviet troops competed with Allied forces under Eisenhower to get to Berlin first. Their path took them through Eastern Europe which, for the duration, had been part of the German Reich but was now to become part of the Soviet bloc. As the Soviet flag was famously raised above the Reichstag (an iconic image captured by a Soviet photographer), a new era began.

The Soviet flag is raised over the Berlin Reichstag on 2 May 1945.

Leader of a superpower

Stalin emerged from the Second World War with enormously enhanced prestige at home and abroad – the architect of the war victory, leading a country that was no longer a pariah but one of the three great Allied powers that would shape the postwar future. To be sure, the victory had been enormously costly, both in terms of damaged infrastructure, military casualties and civilian population loss (a total of well over 20 million dead, although the official Soviet figure – lowered to hide the toll that war had taken – was only 7 million). During the war, some material help had been received from the United States in the form of Lend-lease; and in the first postwar years, UNRRA (an international relief agency created by the Allies in 1943) helped with postwar reconstruction in the western Soviet republics of Ukraine and Belorussia.

In Eastern Europe, the war had secured the all-important buffer. Occupied by the Soviet Army in the final stages of the war, Poland, Hungary, Czechoslovakia and the other Eastern European states all became Soviet satellites, with governments that were more or less Communist. Germany, divided into separate zones of occupation by the Allies for four years after the war, ended up as two countries: the Federal Republic of Germany, consisting of the former Western occupation zones, and the German Democratic Republic, consisting of the former Soviet occupation zone. These were major shifts in the European balance of power; and the popularity of Communist parties in Italy and France raised the possibility that Communist governments might be established there too, via the ballot box. In addition, Communists under Mao were winning the Chinese Civil War, establishing the People's Republic of China in 1949. At war's end, the Soviet Union had been one of three powers (Britain, the United States and the Soviet Union) deciding the fate of the postwar world. By the end of the 1940s, with Britain impoverished and in process of losing its Empire, just two superpowers were left, the United States and the Soviet Union.

It was a dizzying rise in international status for the Soviet Union, but it had a downside: such a major geopolitical realignment naturally produced a counter-reaction. The wartime alliance with Britain and the United States had broken down

Eastern Europe becomes Communist

within a couple of years of the war's end. The former Allies, particularly the United States, were gripped by hysterical alarm at the prospect that Soviet communism was about to conquer the world. In fact, as Stalin well realised, the Soviet Union was in no state to launch a new world war, needing years to rebuild its economy and military. It feared a US attack just as much as the West feared a Soviet one. This fear was particularly acute in the first postwar years, when the US was sole possessor of the atomic bomb, which it had used to end the war with Japan.

The Cold War
takes shape

The half-expected Third World War did not break out in Europe in the postwar years, despite a major confrontation over Berlin in 1948. What emerged, and became steady-state for decades, was a global Cold War in which the Soviet Union and the United States were chief protagonists, each with its own group of supporters throughout the world. The Soviets conceptualized the two camps as the 'capitalist' and 'socialist' worlds. For the Americans, it was 'the free world' versus the world of 'totalitarian dictatorships'. Mutual hostility and suspicion fuelled the Cold War, but it was kept in check by the nuclear threat and the convention that military conflicts would be waged only by proxies. Hostility from and to the West was, of course, nothing new in Soviet terms: it had existed from the moment of the Russian Revolution. What was new was a superpower status that implied parity between the two superpowers, although in fact the United States was stronger.

A cult of Stalin as Leader (*vozhd'*) had grown steadily through the 1930s, as epithets such as 'father of peoples', 'genius', and 'great leader' spread. 'Thank you, comrade Stalin, for our happy childhood' became a popular mantra, with Turkic-speaking Baku housewives going further to thank Stalin for everything in 'our free, bright and smiling life'. In the first half of the thirties, Stalin demurred privately at some of the excessive adulation, but by 1937, he had given in, and the banners that had formerly proclaimed the revolution of 'Marx, Engels and Lenin' celebrated 'Marx, Engels, Lenin and Stalin' instead. Soviet mountaineers placed busts of Stalin on the highest peaks in Central Asia and the Caucasus, with one peak in the Pamir Mountains renamed Mount Stalin. During the war, to go with his new title of 'Generalissimus', propaganda posters captioned 'Stalin leads us to victory!' showed him in Napoleonic guise. By the postwar period, Stalin's pronouncements on all topics, even such esoteric ones as linguistics and economic theory, had the weight of papal encyclicals and had to be cited by all scholars working in the area. Statues and monuments to Stalin shot up everywhere, often on the initiative of local governments, anxious not to be outdone in conspicuous reverence by their neighbours.

Stalin's seventieth birthday in December 1949 pushed the cult over the top. In Moscow, where a giant bust of Stalin was suspended by balloons above the city, international leaders including China's Mao Tse Tung and East Germany's Walter Ulbricht flew in for the lavish celebrations. Trainloads of gifts arrived from the Soviet Union's national republics, the *pièce de résistance* being an enormous rug (70 square metres, weighing 167 kilos) presented by the people of Azerbaijan. There were so many gifts that a special section of the Pushkin Museum was set aside to house them.

The international communist movement was also mobilized to celebrate the seventieth birthday, with the French Communist party sending 'ten trucks decorated with banners' to drive around France to collect birthday presents for Stalin from admirers ranging from war widows to Picasso. The countries of sovietized Eastern Europe vied to outdo each other in gathering letters and gifts from the public to be sent to Stalin; and East Germany's party leadership added a present of their own: a 'state-of-the-art Carl Zeiss planetarium' that was to be built in Stalingrad.

The symbolic gift-giving went two ways. In the immediate postwar years, the city of Moscow had been enhanced by the building of six skyscrapers of wedding-cake design whose design Stalin had personally approved. A similar, but even bigger, wedding-cake building, to be called the Stalin Palace of Culture and Science, was presented to Poland by the Soviet government in April 1952. When completed in 1955, it was the eighth tallest building in the world. Not loved by many Poles, it nevertheless dominated the Warsaw skyline for decades – a visible monument to Stalin and token of the Soviet Union's new towering status in the world.

CHAPTER 2

Stalin's Death

Reports of Stalin's deteriorating health had been circulating since the end of the war. There were rumours that he had had a heart attack. He had cut back progressively on his once very heavy workload and was spending more time each year at resorts in the south. When he was back in Moscow, his office hours were much shorter than before. Associates noticed a decline in stamina, memory loss, abrupt mood swings, and outbursts of anger. Yugoslav Communist Milovan Djilas, visiting Moscow as Tito's representative in 1948 after a three-year interval, was shocked at how much Stalin had aged. Stalin's longtime physician, Dr Vladimir Vinogradov, warned him that he needed to cut back and stop smoking, perhaps think of retiring, at their last meeting in January 1952. In response, Stalin dismissed him, and later had him arrested.

In addition to being old, Stalin was lonely. This was to some extent inherent in his position: for a demi-God there are no equals to be friends. Stalin's wife was dead, his children grown and partially estranged. There were grandchildren, but he rarely saw them. For domestic company, he was dependent on his household servants and bodyguards (particularly the head of his bodyguard, Nikolai Vlasik, and his long-term housekeeper, Valentina Istomina). Politburo members were pressed into service to watch films with him at the Kremlin of an evening, followed by dinners at his dacha where it was compulsory to eat and drink too much and put up with a lot of crude horseplay (Politburo members forced to dance as Stalin watched, tomatoes slipped onto chairs). These excruciating meetings were men-only affairs, in contrast to earlier weekend parties at Stalin's dacha where wives and children were present; they went on until the early morning, for Stalin had become a night owl. Stalin had a whim of iron, and people had to fall into line with his whims for fear of provoking an outburst of anger and suspicion. It was like dealing with a

Long nights at the dacha

crotchety elderly relative, Khrushchev remembered. But this elderly relative's power lay not in the threat of cutting errant family members out of his will but of having his political associates fired, arrested as foreign spies or even executed.

Stalin had always been a suspicious man, whose fear of treachery had sometimes spilled over into paranoia. But his suspicions increased markedly in the postwar years. He was heard to mutter that his old military comrade, Klim Voroshilov, might be a British spy, and Khrushchev remembered him saying, to no one in particular, 'I'm finished. I trust no one, not even myself.' But he still prided himself on his ability to sniff out treachery. He told his Politburo colleagues: 'You are blind like young kittens. What will happen without me? The country will perish because you do not know how to recognize enemies.' Even Politburo members were kept under constant surveillance by the secret police, whose leader answered to Stalin alone. His own personal security and privacy were guarded ever more elaborately. Different unmarked cars took him from Kremlin to dacha, and there was a huge security force on site. But in May 1952 Vlasik, long-time head of Stalin's security team and personally close to his boss, fell out of favour and was arrested a few months later – another empty space in Stalin's life.

Stalin in the mid 1930s with his son, Vasily, and his head of personal security, Nikolai Vlasik, whom he had arrested in December 1952.

Postwar political tensions

Almost all of Stalin's close associates on the Politburo experienced some sort of public rebuff from him in the postwar years. Molotov was slapped down just after the war, following rumours in the Western press that Stalin was ill and Molotov his likely successor. A high-flying recent addition to the Politburo, Nikolai Voznesensky, had a dramatic fall from grace and was executed in the so-called Leningrad affair in 1949. Security chief Beria came under pressure in 1951 through a complex offshoot of Georgian politics known as the Mingrelian affair.

Despite this, paradoxically, the regular business of government continued to be quite efficiently run – just as the home front had been during the war – by the Politburo, which on a day-to-day basis often operated without Stalin. He had become, to a degree, an absentee dictator. But this did not mean that he was out of the picture. He retained his ability to make sudden interventions in any area, cast politicians out of favour, and have them killed. In the areas closest to his heart, which included internal and external security, Gulag, foreign affairs and treatment of nationalities, no Politburo member could risk suggesting policy changes, even if everyone but Stalin tacitly supported them. In these areas of special interest, Stalin might act on his own, overtly or covertly, or have someone else do the legwork under his watchful eye. Sometimes – life in the party was boring without factions! – he might coach a protégé such as young Yuri Zhdanov, Politburo member Andrei's son, on how to play the game of factional politics in the academic sphere.

Andrei Zhdanov, acting as Stalin's surrogate, spearheaded the 'anti-cosmopolitan' campaign, which started after the war as a drive against foreign contacts of all kinds, then focussed on disciplining the Westernizing intelligentsia. Later, without Zhdanov (who had meanwhile died), or any visible direction from the Politburo, it would morph into antisemitism. But in its first years it was xenophobic rather than antisemitic, aimed both at reducing Soviet citizens' foreign contacts in order to make life harder for Western intelligence agencies, and at diminishing Western cultural influence. The United

Anti-cosmopolitan campaign

27

States, represented as the great postwar threat to world peace, was a particular bogey. But this was not, as it might seem, simply a mirror image of American anti-Communism. In the US, anti-Communism was a popular phenomenon as well as governmental policy: ordinary Americans saw Communism as the devil's work and feared the Soviet Union was out to conquer the world. In the Soviet Union, by contrast, attitudes to the United States at the end of the war were quite favourable; and it was exactly these favourable attitudes that the anti-cosmopolitan campaign set out to reverse. The reason Soviet people had to be reminded not to trust the capitalist foreigners, not to marry them (this was expressly forbidden for any Soviet citizen in 1947), and not to admire their culture was because too many of them were doing just that. Stalin's own daughter Svetlana was majoring in American Studies at Moscow State University; her cohort of Soviet university students, including other Politburo children, was wild about American literature (Hemingway), American films, American jazz and American fashion.

The point of the anti-cosmopolitan campaign was to discourage cultural 'servility' and 'bowing and scraping' to the West, particularly by the intelligentsia, and promote a sense of dignity and self-worth in dealing with the outside world. As so often with Stalinist policies, there was a sharp punitive edge. Always alert to the danger of Western spying, Stalin assumed that 'westernizers' in the Soviet cultural world were especially vulnerable to the approaches of Western intelligence agencies. That meant it was best to punish some of them in advance, as a lesson to the others. Noted writers and composers, from the *grande dame* of Russian literature Anna Akhmatova to the erstwhile *enfant terrible* of Soviet music Dmitri Shostakovich, were accordingly subjected to ritual humiliation for succumbing to decadent Western influences. Sergei Prokofiev's Spanish ex-wife Lina, a frequent guest at foreign embassy receptions in Moscow, was sent to Gulag. Stalin's suspicions extended even to Politburo members Molotov and Mikoyan, for whom (as minister of foreign affairs and foreign trade respectively) contact with foreigners was part of the job. At the largely ceremonial Nineteenth Party Congress in

No more bowing and scraping

28

Stalin speaking at the 19th Party Congress in October 1952, where he appeared old and harmless. He was to shock his listeners a few days later at the Party plenum.

October 1952, Stalin uncharacteristically handed over presentation of the Political Report to Malenkov, confining himself to a seven-minute speech of no great import late in the proceedings. But, if that had Politburo members worried for his health and stamina, they had something quite different to worry about at the Party plenum that followed. There, Stalin spoke for over an hour and a half, without notes and with no visible sign of weakness. The content of his speech shocked the assembled delegates. He not only damned Molotov, his closest associate since the early 1920s, and Mikoyan, an old friend from the same period, for sucking up to the Americans, but also suggested that they might be spies. Incongruously (if Stalin had really thought they were spies), they were re-elected to the Politburo (now renamed the Presidium, and doubled in size), but not appointed to a new body that was, in effect, an inner Politburo (the Bureau of the Presidium). At this point, in the words of a Russian historian, 'everyone considered them as good as dead'.

The phenomenon of dead men walking was not unknown in Stalinist politics. But when it had happened before, as in the case of Bukharin at the beginning of the 1930s, it had meant that, as the victim fell ever further from grace, his colleagues silently withdrew from him, breaking whatever personal and social connections existed. Remarkably, in this case, that failed to happen. It was clear that Stalin expected Molotov and Mikoyan to drop out of his social circle; and accordingly his office stopped inviting them to the film showings in the Kremlin and dinner at the dacha. However, the four Politburo heavyweights that were left – Beria, Malenkov, Khrushchev, Nikolai Bulganin (a genial recent addition, Stalin's deputy as Minister for Defence from 1944, then his successor in that post) – treated the banishment of the other two as the whim of an old man that could be disregarded. Informed of dates and times by their colleagues, Molotov and Mikoyan continued to

Gate-crashing the dacha

show up for the evening film screenings – as well as to meetings of the newly formed inner Politburo, where they participated as if they were members. For some months, Stalin did not challenge their presence. Even when they showed up uninvited at his dacha bearing bottles of Georgian wine for the usual celebration of his birthday in December 1952, Stalin accepted their arrival without protest. Afterwards, however, he told the remaining four he had been unhappy about it, and the gate-crashing stopped. This episode is illuminating about Stalin's odd relations with his Politburo. The other Politburo members may have been frightened of him and suspicious of each other, as most historical commentary has emphasized. But they were not so frightened that they felt they had to follow to the letter Stalin's unwritten rule against communication behind his back, and not so mutually suspicious as to be unable to act collectively to subvert his will on occasion.

The subversion would surely not have happened had not *all* Stalin's close associates felt themselves threatened by him at this point, not just Molotov and Mikoyan. This was connect-

From anti-cosmpolitan to antisemitic

ed to the emergence of an antisemitic thrust in the anti-cosmopolitan campaign – a very unwelcome development for the Politburo. Antisemitism was nothing new in Russia and Ukraine – in fact, there had been an upsurge of popular antisemitism in the Army and throughout the country during the Second World War – but it had always been condemned, and frequently punished, by Soviet authorities. Indeed, in deference to this tradition, prosecutions for overt antisemitism continued to be reported in the press in the early 1950s, alongside reports of arrests and dismissals of people with unmistakeably Jewish names that, for the Soviet reader, conveyed the opposite message. Quasi-official sanction of antisemitism was a flagrant departure from Soviet norms. It was domestically risky, both because of the danger of inflaming popular prejudice and its unacceptability to the Soviet intelligentsia, and perverse in terms of foreign policy, given Soviet support of the newly created Jewish state of Israel. On top of that, it had the potential to be used against the Politburo members themselves.

True, with only one Jewish Politburo member (Lazar Kaganovich) out of nineteen, the Soviet party leadership was much less Jewish than it had been in the 1920s, when three of the seven full members had been Jews. But that didn't mean that its members lacked ties to a Jewish milieu. Molotov and Voroshilov had Jewish wives; Malenkov a Jewish son-in-law (as had Stalin at one point); and the social circles in which all of them – and, even more, their children – moved included many Jewish Old Bolsheviks and intellectuals. Jewish connections

Beria, though he had no Jewish family connections, had been instrumental during the war in the setting up of the Jewish Anti-Fascist Committee (JAC), one of whose duties was liaison and fund-raising with the international Jewish community. The JAC was closed down after the war, despite an impressive line-up of Politburo patrons. In 1949, Molotov's wife, Polina Zhemchuzhina, a political figure in her own right, was arrested for Zionism. Malenkov was told to arrange the divorce of his daughter from her Jewish husband, whose grandfather, Solomon Lozovsky, an Old Bolshevik well known to all the Politburo members, had headed the Soviet wartime propaganda agency under which the JAC functioned. In July 1952, Lozovsky and the JAC leaders were put on closed trial for treason and espionage. Remarkably, they defended themselves vigorously in court, but were nevertheless convicted and shot. For those familiar with Stalin's modus operandi, it was all too easy to imagine a follow-up on the lines of the Moscow show trials of the 1930s, with Zhemchuzhina (initially on the list of defendants in the JAC trial, but kept on ice for the time being), Molotov, and other Politburo members in the dock on charges of spying for the Americans, their Jewish connections providing a subtext to mobilise popular indignation.

31

On 13 January 1953, *Pravda* announced the arrest of a number of physicians from the Kremlin Hospital, which treated Politburo members and their families, accompanying this with a lead article headed 'Spies and murderers in the guise of doctors'. The Doctors' Plot, as it came to be known, involved accusations of 'terrorist' attempts on the part of the doctors to kill their patients, allegedly resulting in the death of Politburo member Andrei Zhdanov in 1948. They were also charged with espionage for Western intelligence agencies. Among the accused was Dr Vinogradov, personal physician to Stalin and to a number of other Politburo members, who had made the rash suggestion that Stalin should think of retiring; he was said to have been a long-standing agent of British intelligence. Vinogradov was ethnically Russian, but almost all other arrested men were Jewish (as was evident to Soviet readers from their names and patronymics). The American Jewish Joint Distribution Committee, a charity helping Jews worldwide and in contact with the JAC during the war, was specifically mentioned as the doctors' conduit to US intelligence.

Doctors' Plot

This appears to have been purely a Stalin initiative, cooked up with people in the security police (not Beria, but his enemies in the organization). Interrogation was ongoing, readers were told. That meant, in effect, script-writing for possible trials, whose nature can be guessed from the (unpublished) fact that Zhemchuzhina was brought in from exile in Kazakhstan for further cross-examination. Politburo members were appalled at the announcement of the Doctors' Plot, and had panicky discussions about it among themselves. 'We knew these people personally because they had once treated us,' Khrushchev said later. But it was not just a matter of personal concern for their family doctors. Left out of the loop in the run-up to the Doctors' Plot, the Politburo members had good reason to feel themselves in danger.

If the announcement of the Doctors' Plot frightened the top political elite and the intelligentsia, it had a different impact on the broader Soviet public. By February 1953, people all over the country were refusing to be treated by Jewish doctors for fear of being poisoned, while Moscow was buzzing with rumours of the imminent deportation to the Soviet hinterland of all Jews as a group. This would actually have been a difficult exercise, given that, unlike the Chechens and other ethnic groups deported during the war, they were geographically dispersed; and there is nothing in the archives to show that such an operation was in fact planned. Those same archives, however, contain ample evidence that a mass action against the Jews would have been popular with many non-Jewish Soviet citizens, who saw Jews as a privileged white-collar group with disproportionate access to good apartments and prestigious jobs.

Death at the dacha

The last of the compulsory heavy-drinking dinners at Stalin's dacha took place on Saturday, 28 February 1953. As Khrushchev later remembered, it was nothing special. The invited group (now reduced in size, since Molotov and Mikoyan had stopped coming) got back to Moscow, as usual, in the early hours of the morning. The next day, Sunday 1 March, Khrushchev was surprised not to receive any phone calls or summonses from the Boss: it was rare that Stalin, without family, friends or hobbies to occupy him, allowed a close associate an uninterrupted day off. Only after Khrushchev had finally gone to bed did the phone ring – and then it was Malenkov, reporting that household personnel from the dacha had just contacted him with concerns about Stalin's health.

Stalin falls ill

Two eye-witness reports exist of what happened at Stalin's dacha between 1 March and his death on the 5th, and these are the basis of all subsequent accounts. The reports come from Khrushchev and from Stalin's daughter, Svetlana Alliluyeva. Written a decade or more after the event, they are notable for their similarity in some colourful details (Khrushchev may have read Svetlana's book, and had certainly heard extracts from it on foreign radio by the time he dictated his own memoirs). Both present Beria in the worst possible light. This is not surprising: in the years between Stalin's death and Khrushchev's recording of his memories, Beria had been executed, on Khrushchev's initiative, and had become the universal scapegoat, while Svetlana, still trying to think the

33

best of her father despite damning accusations against him in 1956, needed the fall guy that Beria's disgrace provided (more on this in chapters 3 and 5). But it does make it hard to be sure what actually happened, given that the only counter-narrative – from Beria's son, reporting what his father had told him many years earlier – is second-hand. What is clear in all accounts is that, with Stalin incapacitated, Beria immediately took charge, and the rest of the Politburo followed his lead without overt protest.

Beria takes charge

Stalin lived alone at his dacha, though with a massive entourage for his protection – more than 300 security personnel plus seventy-three servants. All this availed him little, however, because when he didn't emerge one day, his protectors were all too frightened to go and see what had happened. Stalin was a late riser, but even so the guards and household personnel became uneasy by the afternoon of 1 March, when there was no sign of life from his private quarters. Then, around 6 p.m., his light went on, and everyone breathed a sigh of relief, although they found it odd that he didn't call anybody for duties. There was discussion among the bodyguards about going in to check on him, but Stalin jealously guarded his privacy, and nobody wanted to be the man to arouse his ire by disturbing it. Vlasik, the former head of the bodyguards and on closer terms with Stalin, might have risked it, but he was under arrest.

Finally they sent in the housekeeper, Valentina Istomina. She found Stalin semi-conscious on the floor, unable to speak or move his right hand, and having wet himself. Stroke would have been the obvious diagnosis, even for a layman, but the guards were stymied both by the involuntary urination (Stalin would be furious to have been seen in a humiliating position) and the fact that his personal physician, Dr Vinogradov, was, like Vlasik, in prison and therefore unavailable. They picked Stalin up, put him on the divan, and called Malenkov, as head of the government, for advice. Malenkov summoned the rest of the inner group (Khrushchev, Beria, Bulganin), and they hurried out to the dacha in the early hours of the morning. But they too were frightened of provoking an outburst of anger, individually or collectively, if Stalin woke up and found

Paralysed by fear

them invading his private space. After Beria and Malenkov crept in together to have a look at him, Malenkov having first removed squeaky new shoes, it was decided that, after all, Stalin was now apparently sleeping, so no immediate action was required. They all returned to the city.

The room in the dacha at Kuntsevo where Stalin died. His death mask is on display.

Early the next morning, the guards called again: the sleep looked unnatural, was it perhaps (after more than twelve hours) time to call in a doctor? But even that was not simple: which doctor, when all those they knew from the Kremlin Hospital had been arrested in the Doctors' Plot? Soviet Health Minister Tretyakov was asked to provide a list of (Russian) doctors who might be suitable, and secret police interrogators pulled Dr Yakov Rapoport, one of the arrested Kremlin doctors, out of his prison cell to get his assessment of their abilities. Rapoport didn't know why they were asking, but took some malicious pleasure in telling them that all the doctors on the list were mediocre. Instead he recommended a number of better specialists, mainly Jewish, who were all, like him, under arrest. Some (Russian) doctors were finally found and arrived at the dacha on the morning of 2 March. They approached Stalin gingerly, hesitating even to touch him to check for a pulse. 'You're a doctor, aren't you?... Take hold of his hand properly,' Beria exploded.

The situation at the dacha was settling into the black comedy vein that Armando Iannucci would brilliantly exploit seven decades later in his film *The Death of Stalin*. Finally the doctors pulled themselves together enough to agree on a stroke diagnosis, with poor prognosis, and the death watch vigil began. Sometimes all four of the inner circle were present, but, for purposes of mutual protection, never less than two (Malenkov and Beria on the day shift, and Khrushchev and Bulganin on the night one). Klim Voroshilov and Lazar Kaganovich were summoned, as old friends and (lesser) Politburo members. So were Molotov and Mikoyan, whose invitation may have been a gesture of prudence (if, God forbid, questions were later raised about the death, best to make sure all interested parties were there and equally compromised) but also constituted an implicit annulment of Stalin's ban on them.

Bedside scenes

Stalin's daughter Svetlana was called to the scene, as was her brother Vasily. He, as usual, was drunk, and wandered around saying to nobody in particular, 'They've killed him.' In Svetlana's version, several of her Politburo 'uncles' (Khrushchev, Bulganin) embraced her in tears, and she saw most of the rest (Voroshilov, Kaganovich, Malenkov) weeping at one point or other. She wept herself, of course, and so did Stalin's household servants, particularly Istomina. Beria did not weep, but, back in Moscow, his wife did: she felt sorry for Stalin, she said, such a lonely man. Khrushchev later admitted shedding tears, and said he was 'very sorry we were losing Stalin'. But, he added, 'I wasn't just weeping for Stalin. I was terribly worried about the future of the Party and the future of the country.' That was undoubtedly a sentiment all the leaders present shared.

A notable feature of both Svetlana's and Khrushchev's accounts was the loathsome behaviour of Beria, who was 'spewing hatred against [Stalin] and mocking him' – but, whenever Stalin showed signs of returning to consciousness, throwing himself on his knees and kissing his hand (though this must be taken with a grain of salt, given the interest of both in blackening Beria). In fact, only one instance of apparent return to consciousness is cited, when Stalin raised his left arm with what Svetlana remembered as a terrible expression on his face, perhaps trying to curse his fate. Khrushchev noticed this too, but as he interpreted it, Stalin – whom an attendant was attempting to spoon feed at the time – was pointing at a picture of a girl feeding a lamb on the wall above him (one of several sentimental images recently cut out of one of the Soviet weeklies by Stalin); and what he was trying to say was that he and the lamb were now in the same boat. (That version, shedding an odd light on both Stalin and Khrushchev, did not make it into the movie.)

Here we must make a sudden swerve from the black comedy genre. Stalin's associates may have seemed hapless bumblers in their early handling of the situation at the dacha, as Iannucci's film memorably shows. But the real crisis they faced was a political one, organizing the transition after Stalin's death, and this – departing abruptly from Iannucci's script – they handled brilliantly. Quickly setting up an efficient government, headed by themselves as 'the collective leadership', they not only achieved a smooth transition but also very rapidly jettisoned key aspects of Stalin's legacy (of which more in chapter 3). No wonder Iannucci didn't include this in his film. Stalin himself might have been surprised – though perhaps, bearing in mind his comrades' sterling performance on the wartime home front, when he was off worrying about the military side, he shouldn't have been.

Smooth transition

Stalin's successors – the Politburo members out at his dacha for the death – may have already conferred about the political future in a neighbouring room as Stalin lay dying. They certainly convened in the Kremlin on 10.40 am on 2 March, with Molotov and Mikoyan restored to the inner group and Pravda's editor and various other top officials in attendance. The meeting place, the Politburo's usual one, was Stalin's office, with Stalin's chair remaining empty as a token of respect. There, having already put out a press release on Stalin's illness within hours of the terminal diagnosis, they prepared the notice that would go out on his death (which had not yet happened). They also finalized the composition of the new government. Despite Beria's conspicuous assumption of leadership at the dacha, he was not to head it: Malenkov was. (According to his son, Beria ruled himself out because you couldn't have two Georgians in succession running Russia, and he thought he could dominate Malenkov.) Beria would be

Malenkov appointed head of government

in charge of the secret police, Bulganin of the Army, Molotov of foreign affairs, and Mikoyan of trade, while Khrushchev would continue as party secretary (now in effect first secretary) – in other words, much the same division of responsibilities as had existed in the past. On 5 March, with Stalin still alive but doctors saying his death was unavoidable, the composition of the new government was officially approved at a joint meeting of the party's Central Committee and the Soviet state's Council of Ministers. In another act of deference or wariness, Stalin's name remained on the roster of Politburo members, although he was no longer listed as General Secretary of the party.

The funeral

On message: the Soviet front pages after Stalin's death on 5 March. 1953.

Stalin died on the evening of the day the new government was announced, at 9.50 p.m. His body lay in state to be viewed at the Hall of Columns in Moscow for three days, with the public filing past – 'hurried and jostled, sixteen abreast', as an American correspondent remembered, '... forced at a half-trot past the bier'. As the official footage shows, some women and even a few military men were weeping, but most, looking sideways back at the bier as they passed it, simply seemed concentrated and wary. In the roped-off inner circle, Svetlana stood in silent grief. The Politburo members were photographed, standing sombrely by the coffin, four or on each side, their thoughts inscrutable. Voroshilov and Bulganin were in military uniform, but the rest wore civilian suits with red armbands bordered with black on their left arms. Their children, awed by death and respectfully devoted to Stalin, came to pay their last respects. Sergo Mikoyan was there every day, and Sergo Beria came several times (the Politburo was a tribe: both young men were named for Stalin's fellow Georgian, friend and Politburo colleague of the 1930s, 'Sergo' Ordzhonikidze).

The Hall of Columns was filled with classical music as Stalin lay in state. The best Soviet musicians including David Oistrakh, the Bolshoi Theatre Opera and Choir, and the Beethoven Quartet were there, performing in shifts, to play Tchaikovsky and Mozart's Requiem. A classical music critic would have given the occasion high marks, although an anonymous letter-writer complained that, with most of the musicians being Jews, the music sounded 'insincere'. (This was inaccurate as well as unfair: in response to the anti-cosmopolitan campaign, a hasty recruitment of Russians to choirs and orchestras had brought the Jewish share of musicians down to 36 per cent.) Some of the performers had been ferried across town, not without difficulty, from their earlier gig at the House of Composers for the funeral of Sergei Prokofiev, who had died on the same day as Stalin.

Crowds in Moscow on the day of Stalin's funeral, 9 March 1953.

Movement was difficult because Moscow was cordoned off, as it always was for big public holidays, with railway movement restricted and security troops stationed in the centre. But people poured into the city anyway when they heard the news of Stalin's death. Russian memoirs generally represent this in terms of popular patriotic longing for a last sight of the dead leader. But a visiting Czech Communist, Zdenek Mlynar, waiting in line at the Hall of Columns with his friend and fellow student at Moscow University, Mikhail Gorbachev, remembered it in more carnivalesque terms, as 'a crowd united by determination not to miss a spectacle, whether it be a funeral or a public execution', many with bottles of vodka in their pockets. The crush produced the major glitch of an otherwise well-handled and decorous funeral. The crowd in the small streets near the Hall of Columns, made narrower by the police trucks parked there to preserve order, panicked, and over a hundred people were trampled to death. The episode was hidden from the public at the time, but the news still went round on the grapevine, with the usual exaggerations of numbers. 'The ominous words, "Khodynka... Khodynka" spread through the city,' an observer remembered. This recalled a similar incident that had occurred on Khodynka Field in 1896, when hundreds hoping to receive a gift on the occasion of the coronation of Emperor Nicholas II were killed in the crush.

What's in a hat? Malenkov (left) and Beria (right) lead the pallbearers.

On 9 March, the coffin, covered in red cloth, was closed and the cortege made its dignified way to Lenin's Mausoleum, accompanied by the strains of Chopin's Funeral March. The Politburo members served as pall bearers, Beria first on the left side of the coffin, Malenkov first on the right. All were in winter overcoats and (but for Beria) Russian fur hats, pudgy Malenkov's being a curly Persian lamb affair which, unkind commentators suggested, made him look like a woman. The intense cold of the first days of the funeral period had passed, snow had melted from the ground, and there was even a light spring rain as the cortege slowly covered the short distance from the Hall of Columns, next to the Bolshoi Theatre, to Red Square. One name, LENIN, had always been inscribed above the entrance to the Mausoleum. Now it was LENIN on top and STALIN (one letter longer, so taking up a bit more room) below.

Malenkov addresses the crowd in front of the mausoleum, henceforth to house both Lenin and Stalin.

The parapet running along the top of the Mausoleum had always been a favourite spot for leaders to greet the people on occasions like Revolution Day. For the funeral, the new leaders stood in their accustomed positions there, except that Stalin was not, as usual, in the middle. In the funeral orations, Malenkov spoke, rather unexpectedly, of peace, and Beria of the rule of law, neither devoting much time to the deceased. Molotov, former disgrace forgotten, was the only one to speak of Stalin as an old friend. Beria struck an interesting sartorial note with his black homburg, a striking contrast to the others' Russian fur hats. It was the same type of hat that Dwight Eisenhower had just worn, flouting convention, at his inauguration as President of the United States in Washington.

41

But if Beria (and Malenkov) were trying to send a message, Washington, as we shall see, failed to receive it.

Washington's own message on Stalin's death, sent on 5 March 1953, was as dry as official protocol could make it: 'the government of the United States tenders its official condolences to the government of the U.S.S.R. on the death of Generalissimo Joseph Stalin, Prime Minister of the Soviet Union'. To be sure, this looks almost fulsome compared to the Vatican's response. Calling on Roman Catholics to pray for Stalin's soul, Pope Pius XII noted dryly that Stalin had 'arrived at the end of his arid life and must account to the Almighty for his actions'.

The Communist bloc countries marked the death with the same zeal with which they had celebrated Stalin's seventieth birthday. In Romania, the state organized its own funeral ceremony for Stalin in Bucharest; churches held special services, and crowds lined up outside the Soviet Embassy to sign the condolence book. East Berlin went into full mourning, with German citizens piling tier upon tier of floral wreaths at the base of Stalin's statue. In France, the government declared three days of official mourning, and factories observed fifteen minutes of silence at the moment of Stalin's interment. In India, where national and state parliaments adjourned as a token of respect, and flags were lowered on all government buildings, Prime Minister Jawaharlal Nehru described Stalin as 'a man who, such as few do, moulded the destinies of his age', and hoped that 'the world may be excited by this event into thinking more in terms of peace' - in other words, that the death might make it easier to end the Cold War. Judging by Malenkov's funeral speech, at least some of Stalin's successors had the same hope.

CHAPTER 3

Reactions at Home

A still from official footage shot in March 1953 for *The Great Farewell*. Intended to glorify Stalinism, the film was canned, likely for political reasons, and first screened only in 1991, after the fall of the USSR.

Everyone later remembered that they had wept on hearing of Stalin's death, and that most others around them had wept too, in a community of grief. Surveying Russian memoirs, Irina Paperno notes that it was 'a moment of intense collective emotion... There is hardly a text that does not describe 5 March 1953, and hardly a text that does not mention crying at the news of Stalin's death'. 'The whole of Russia wept,' the young poet Yevgeny Yevtushenko wrote. 'So did I. We wept sincerely with grief and perhaps also with fear for the future. At a writers' meeting, poets read out their poems in Stalin's honour, their voices broken by sobs.' The weepers were not only people who would later be called Stalinists, but also leading cultural reformers such as Alexander Tvardovsky, and even intellectuals who, being prisoners at the time, heard the news of Stalin's death in prison or Gulag. Future dissident and memoirist Lev Kopelev remembered 'sharing [his] genuine grief with both other prisoners and guards'. Another future memoirist, Evgeniya Ginzburg, hearing the news on the radio in Gulag, 'collapsed, sobbing loudly'. Lina Prokofieva was weeping in Gulag at the same time, but not for Stalin. The death that mattered to her was that of her ex-husband, Sergei Prokofiev (picked up by a fellow prisoner on the radio).

Shock was the other reaction to Stalin's death that people recalled. It felt like the 'death of God' to many people – a momentous, almost incomprehensible event for which no previous experience had prepared them. People who had grown up believing that Stalin was taking care of them felt lost: 'Who will look after us now?' To Raisa Orlova, Kopelev's future wife, it was 'a disaster... the end'. The writer Ilya Ehrenburg 'feared the worst'. But along with the shock and fear was some underlying feeling of liberation. Sergo Beria, one of the guards of honour at Stalin's funeral, sensed 'a feeling of relief' among those around him. American journalist Harrison Salisbury observed 'a numb sense of shock' of the kind which 'a workhorse might feel which for twenty years had been hitched to shafts of a heavy cart and, suddenly, the leather harness dropped off'.

'Who will look after us now?'

The writer Andrei Sinyavsky was put in mind of dogs rather than workhorses in his satirical novella of late Stalinism, *The Trial Begins*:

> The Master was dead.
> The town seemed empty as a desert. You feel like sitting on your haunches, lifting up your head, and howling like a homeless dog.
> Dogs who have lost their masters stray about the earth and sniff the air in anguish. They never bark, they only growl... They wait, they are forever waiting, gazing, longing: 'Come! Come and feed me! Come and kick me! Beat me as much as you like (but not too hard, if you please), Only come!'

Reactions and reassessments

Russia's new leaders were not howling in the desert; rather, according to an experienced British Russia-watcher, they were 'blossoming like leathery cacti'. They showed no nostalgia for their days of servitude. How devoted they had been to Stalin in his difficult last years is debatable. Molotov, Kaganovich and Voroshilov seem to have retained their old personal attachment and respect, but both Beria and Mikoyan astonished their sons by disclosing their *lack* of affection, still less veneration (though Sergo Beria had already found this out in conversation with his father in the early 1950s, when Lavrenty gave him instructions on what to do in the event of his (Lavrenty's) arrest.

'It stunned me to learn that Stalin was preparing to get rid of my father. "Doesn't he realise that you are devoted to him?" I stammered. "Where did you get the idea that I was devoted to him?" he replied.'

For Stepan Mikoyan, a 30-year-old test pilot, disillusionment came just after Stalin's death, when, thinking to impress his father with his own devotion, he told him he had gone every day to the Hall of Columns where Stalin lay in state. 'You were wasting your time,' Anastas responded.

Molotov never disclosed similar thoughts, but it is hard to believe that relief was not part of his private reaction to Stalin's passing. 'If Stalin was dying a natural death it was the luckiest thing that had ever happened to the men who stood closest to him,' Harrison Salisbury thought to himself, standing in line at the Central Telegraph Office to file his copy on Stalin's last illness. The journalist was not alone in wondering if Stalin died a natural death – indeed, it is clear that the leaders, keeping vigil at his deathbed always in pairs, were guarding against such questions and possible accusations. When Molotov was asked late in life if it was possible that Beria had killed Stalin, he agreed in principle; and even claimed that Beria muttered to him, as they stood together on the Mausoleum at the first May Day celebrations after Stalin's death, 'I got rid of him... I saved you all'. It seems an unusual moment to choose for a confession, all the odder given Molotov's known loyalty to Stalin. Pavel Sudoplatov, a senior member of the Stalinist secret police, later summarily dismissed rumours that Beria had organized Stalin's murder as 'impossible'. Stalin's colleagues watching over him at the dacha as he lay unconscious, might, of course, have acted in concert, like the passengers in Agatha Christie's *Murder on the Orient Express* – but surely someone would have ratted in the end, or tried to pin the blame on someone else. The (perhaps disappointed)

'I saved you all'

45

consensus of historians is that there is no evidence that Beria or anyone else killed Stalin.

Rumours of foul play circulated regardless, as after every prominent death in Russia. Even an insider like the writer Konstantin Simonov confessed that 'a quarter of a century after the event I am still tormented by curiosity as to how he really died'. People doubted that they had been given the true, or at least the full, story. The public announcement, stating that Stalin had died in the Kremlin when he had actually died at the dacha, contained a pointless inaccuracy that the rumour mill quickly picked up. There was speculation about murder – but initial rumours did not, as one might expect, suggest that Stalin's successors were to blame. Instead, logically given the recent publicity about the Doctors' Plot, fingers were pointed at the 'usual suspects' – Jews and doctors. It was 'the hand of the Jews', ordinary citizens wrote in – usually but not always anonymously – to the party Central Committee. The 'killer doctors... must have given him poisonous medications that release their poison over time,' one surmised in explanation of the time lapse between their doctors' arrest and Stalin's death.

The public also sent in suggestions about how to memorialize Stalin: a Pantheon, perhaps; giving the city of Moscow Stalin's name; or even renaming the USSR 'the Union of Soviet *Stalinist* Republics' instead of 'Socialist'. Some people wrote in with thoughts about the succession. Molotov, the oldest and best-known of the leaders, prime minister for many years, was the favoured candidate: 'Why don't you become our Leader?' an admirer wrote. 'We ordinary people all wanted to see you in the place of Joseph Vissarionovich.' Beria and Malenkov received some negative votes on the ground that they were probably Jewish (they weren't). Some concerned citizens wrote to the Central Committee warning against faction-fighting over the succession, expressing fear of sparking another 'time of troubles' like that of the seventeenth-century interregnum, whose ill fame lived on in popular imagination.

Not everybody went along with the conventional pieties. 'For a dog, a dog's death' shows up frequently in the prosecutors' files for early 1953, along with such comments as 'Stalin died: now we have one less selfish bastard'. Women weeping at the news were sometimes upbraided with a curt 'Stop snivelling' or 'Is it your son that died?' Many Stalin-haters cited collectivization as the reason for their dislike, but the nationalities question also surfaced, as in the joke circulating in Lithuania that Stalin had directed that his heart be buried in Georgia and his brain in Moscow, and that 'another body part' be chopped into sixteen pieces, 'to be given to each of the sixteen republics so that... he wouldn't have died leaving nothing to the people'.

Hearts, brains and other body parts

New directions

Nobody expected immediate, radical policy changes. After all, the new leaders were Stalin's men – 'party hacks' in the judgement of Western observers – who for decades had been subordinate to Stalin, responsive to his every command, apparently devoid of independence or personal initiative. Under close surveillance, aware of Stalin's ultra-sensitivity to any sign of mutiny, the members of Stalin's Politburo would surely have had no chance to confer covertly with each other in his last years about succession or any other substantive issue. Clearly they would need time, after Stalin's death, to assess the new situation and decide what, if any, policy changes were appropriate.

Reasonable though those assumptions were, they turned out to be wrong. Not only did the successors have a new government set up before Stalin was even dead, they also had a raft of radical policy changes ready within weeks, with more initiatives following in the months that followed. The substantive policy changes introduced in short order by the 'collective leadership', as Stalin's successors called themselves, are comparable with those of Khrushchev's Thaw and Gorbachev's perestroika – with the important difference that in 1953, the reforms were carried through without open public discussion, and the leadership did not wave a banner of reform. This reticence no doubt reflected a wish to preserve an ambiguous relationship with Stalin's legacy to avoid provoking a backlash. Beria, the most radical reformer of the group, seems to have been keener than the others at getting

Swift and radical reform

47

the reform message out. When his wife reproached him for the lack of emotion in his speech at Stalin's funeral, saying that 'people won't understand', he answered, 'On the contrary, I hope they *will* understand me' – meaning understand that he was proposing to lead the way in a new direction. There is no indication that this message got through to the Soviet public, however; the security chief was probably not, in most people's minds, a likely initiator of reform.

The first major policy change to come down the pike, within three weeks of Stalin's death, was the announcement of a mass amnesty for non-political prisoners in Gulag. For years Beria had wanted a major downsizing of Gulag, which he considered an economically irrational form of labour, but it was a question on which Stalin was adamant. Evidently there was a silent consensus among the other Politburo members that Beria was right and that Gulag had grown impossibly large. The proposal for an amnesty was presented by Beria on 24 March 1953, and three days later a decree was approved

Release of Gulag prisoners

freeing over a million prisoners immediately. Most political prisoners had to wait for individual scrutiny of their dossiers, but some started to emerge. First out was Molotov's wife Polina Zhemchuzhina, brought back from exile two days after Stalin's funeral and theatrically presented by Beria to Molotov as a birthday gift (Molotov had turned sixty-three on the day of Stalin's funeral).

Next in line was the sensational withdrawal of charges against the Kremlin doctors and their release from prison, announced in *Pravda* on 4 April. They were wholly innocent, the announcement from Beria's security service stated, and their confessions had been obtained with illegal methods of interrogation (meaning torture) for which the offending officers had been arrested. There could not have been a clearer signal, both that the antisemitic campaign of Stalin's last years was over, and that the security police was to be reined in.

The Stalin cult came to an abrupt halt, with almost all mention of his name, including the formerly omnipresent use of the adjective 'Stalinist' to describe any Soviet achievement or initiative, dropped from the newspapers. The habit of ubiquitous quotation of Stalin's obiter dicta stopped, and

Pravda's front page on 6 April 1953. The headline, above a lengthy article about the false accusation of the Jewish doctors, translates as: 'Soviet socialist legality is inviolable'.

the ongoing publication of his collected works was halted. The impact must have been shocking on a population where nobody under forty had known a time when Stalin's name was not conspicuously venerated. The change was the more striking because it reversed the practice of the previous succession back in the 1920s, when, far from downplaying the memory of the dead leader, Stalin and the other contenders had sought to attach themselves to Lenin's coattails. The burgeoning Stalin cult had not only played off the popular cult of Lenin that had arisen on his death in 1924 but also emphasized Stalin's close ties with his mentor. Something very different was going on now.

Nationalities policy underwent an equally dramatic change of direction, with an abrupt reversal of the tendency towards russification that had marked Stalin's last years. Beria again took the lead, but a somewhat milder version of his policies was continued after his ousting in June 1953. Starting with the Baltic republics, where the postwar appointment of Russians to top positions had caused much dissatisfaction, Russian officials were summarily dismissed and replaced by natives of the republic. It was the same, if a bit less frenzied, throughout the non-Russian Soviet world. On 12 June 1953, the party leaders ordered the recall of all senior officials sent from Moscow to the republics who did not speak the local language; the transfer of all government correspondence from Russian to the local language; and the requirement that first secretaries of republican communist parties be natives, not Russian carpet-baggers.

Economic changes, although acknowledged to be necessary, took longer to plan and were harder to achieve. On 1 April 1953 the new leaders began with sharp reductions in retail prices. This was a tried and tested crowd-pleaser, but not a policy likely to serve the broader aim, promoted particularly by Malenkov, of increasing the supply and variety of consumer goods. True, telling the public that steel plants and mines would no longer have absolute priority in Soviet budgets was a shift of some significance, but implementation was patchy in the 1950s. There was some improvement in living standards in the first couple of years after Stalin's death, notably in provision of housing stock (in chronically short supply in the big industrial cities), textiles, and foodstuffs like eggs and meat, but it fell short of Plan targets.

Five a day! Soviet leaders tuck in at the Vegetable Growing pavilion at the 1954 All-Russian Agricultural Exhibition. Left to right: Khrushchev, Malenkov, Voroshilov and the exhibition director, Nikolai Tsitsin.

One of the obstacles to improving urban living standards was the woeful condition of agriculture. The collective farms had been mercilessly squeezed by their monopoly customer, the state, ever since collectivization; and their abolition remained the impossible dream of many Soviet malcontents. The new leaders were not ready for change of that magnitude (any more than Khrushchev would be in 1956 or Gorbachev thirty years later). But substantive measures to lighten the burden on the peasantry – a lowering of taxes on the collective farmers, together with a raising of prices on the goods they produced and sold to the state – were quickly introduced. These, however, would not necessarily increase output, which was key to raising living standards in the towns. The hope was that that would be accomplished via a dramatic expansion of acreage under cultivation for grain crops, the 'Virgin Lands' programme associated with Khrushchev's name, but initiated in 1954 under the collective leadership.

Poor though the output of the consumer and agricultural sides of the economy was in the last years of Stalin's rule, there had at least been substantial rebuilding of the industrial sector after its wartime pulverization. Not so in the realm of culture, from which life seemed to be ebbing away fast. The 'conflictlessness' of Soviet society was an ideological tenet in vogue during the late Stalin period which, as applied to Soviet art, had alarmingly negative consequences: novels and films without conflict turned out to be deadly dull. There was general agreement that, as a result of strict censorship and emphasis on the 'production' novel ('boy meets tractor'), Soviet literature had become boring and mediocre. In cinema, it was even worse – a combination of censorship and production difficulties meant that the *total* production of Soviet films (excluding filmed versions of theatre productions) in 1951 amounted to seven in 1951 and eleven in 1952, as compared with hundreds coming out of Hollywood each year.

Cultural desert

The autumn of 1953 – six months after Stalin's death – has been described as the first 'wild moment' of cultural thaw, when 'everyone suddenly started singing, at first tentatively, then, in a rush, as a full dawn chorus'. A major stimulus was the literary journal *Novy Mir*, edited by Alexander Tvardovsky, which in 1954 published the Ilya Ehrenburg novella that gave the Thaw (*Ottepel'*) its name. 'Sincerity' (in place of enforced conformity) was the watchword of this movement, and while the concept did embrace truth-telling on social questions, its main focus initially was on emotional openness – more lyric poetry, and plays whose characters were people and not ideological stereotypes. Ehrenburg's novella, set in

The Thaw is published

51

Boy meets girl meets machine. *Encounter of a Lifetime* (*Navstrechu Zhizny*), one of just eleven feature films made in the USSR in 1952, is set in a Leningrad machine-tooling factory.

Навстречу жизни

the transitional period from the winter of 1953 to the spring of 1954, was not rated highly by critics but had sensational success with the public. Its characters live boring, unfulfilled lives before they fall in love and, after setbacks, walk off into new lives as spring (the post-winter thaw) quickens.

The new leaders were in favour of cultural thaw – but not too much of it, not too fast, and within certain parameters of Soviet decency. 'We... were scared - really scared,' Khrushchev remembered. 'We were afraid the thaw might unleash a flood, which we wouldn't be able to control and which could drown us... wash away all the barriers and retaining walls of our society'. So Ehrenburg got slapped down, and *Novy Mir*'s editors got fired - but these were only temporary setbacks. When English journalist Edward Crankshaw returned to the Soviet Union in 1955, having read about the supposed death of Soviet cultural reform in the Western press, he 'was deeply struck by the unquestioning confidence of writers and painters and musicians that the Thaw was still going on, and would go on'.

The cultural Thaw was important to the intelligentsia, which supported the new leaders' stance while pressing them to go further. Ordinary citizens, on the other hand, tended to be more interested in improvement of living standards, where the new policies earned some credit for good intentions but also complaints that results were not quick enough. It would be a mistake, however, to assume – as Western commentators often do – that reforms, being self-evidently good, necessarily went down well with the Soviet public. There were aspects of the post-Stalin leadership's radical change of direction, including some particularly approved by Western commentators, that large sections of the Soviet public actively disliked.

The first wave of adverse reaction came with the release of the Jewish doctors on 3 April 1953. In *Pravda*'s mailbox for 8–9 April 1953, only fourteen out of fifty-two writers welcomed the release, while the rest expressed 'doubts and confusion'. One letter implicitly questioned the new leaders' own loyalty, noting that 'when Stalin, defender of the people, died, they immediately released the spies', that is, the Jewish doctors. Another wrote: 'You think you will change our views on Jews. No, you won't change them. Jews were parasites in our eyes, and remain so. They push us Russians out of all cultural institutions, they don't take on heavy work, they don't plough the soil.' A third took a different tack: 'How many innocent victims of repressions of 1933–4 and 1937–8 are still in camps, but they are not the ones who are released as first priority, but rather a handful of Jews. Russians are insulted, Jews protected'. 'What does it mean to free those enemies, the professor-murderers?' wrote one citizen to Molotov.' It amounted to 'blackening Comrade Stalin', since he had sanctioned the arrests.

An even greater cause of dissatisfaction was the Gulag amnesty – or rather, its consequences, namely the release of thousands of former prisoners with criminal records onto the streets without housing or jobs. The public panic started in the

Jewish doctors released

53

areas closest to camps in the north and far east of the country, like Magadan, where released prisoners 'gathered in the city's park of culture and rest to drink and fight, terrorizing the city'; but spread as the released prisoners fanned out along the railway lines into different regions. By summer, the public was in a state of high alarm about an urban crime wave that

Crime wave

included murders, rapes, armed break-ins and drunken fights at railway stations, all attributed to the released prisoners. This was not just hysteria: the number of crimes registered in the Soviet Union in 1953 was more than twice the previous year, and 'police repeatedly found themselves outnumbered and over-powered in the face of rampaging groups of return-ees'. In Moscow, people were said to be afraid of going out in the evenings because of the 'criminal-recidivists, degenerates, the dregs of humanity' who had appeared on their streets. Stalin would have had more sense than to allow this, many reasoned. It was a blot, albeit a fairly temporary one, on the collective leadership's efforts to project an image of stability and competence.

Ousting of Beria

The summer of 1953 was a time of crisis for Stalin's successors. The principle of collective leadership had genuine supporters within the group. Neither Molotov, who in terms of seniority and popular expectation could have aspired to be no. 1, nor Malenkov, whose position as prime minister led Western observers to assume he had similar hopes, seems to have had ambitions for personal primacy. But there were two members of the group, Beria and Khrushchev, who did have their eyes on the top job. Beria, heading the secret police, led the pack as a reformer but annoyed the other members of the leadership by claiming all the credit and behaving more and more abrasively, even contemptuously, towards them. Khrushchev, a junior member of the leadership, little known to the public outside Ukraine (where he had been party secretary before moving to Moscow), was not at first considered a serious contender. His folksy self-presentation and genial demeanour made it easy to underestimate his ambition, resourcefulness and ruthlessness. His colleagues should also have remembered that his position as party secretary had been Stalin's springboard to power thirty years earlier.

Beria, for all his lauded cunning, seems to have been totally taken aback when, on 26 June 1953, Khrushchev ambushed him at a leadership meeting in the Kremlin. He was first berated by his colleagues for arrogance and his handling of the workers' revolt in East Germany, and then, to his astonishment (he initially thought it was a joke), put under arrest Beria is arrested and removed by Marshal Georgy Zhukov. Conspiratorially summoned by Khrushchev, Zhukov had been waiting outside with a small military unit in case of need, but in fact Beria offered no resistance. The arrest was Khrushchev's idea, but the rest of the leaders went along, probably both because they thought Beria had got too big for his boots and because they were afraid that, in his capacity as security head, he had compromising material on all of them. Mikoyan, who supported Beria's removal as head of the security police, had thought the plan was to put him in charge of the oil industry. Molotov, who had clashed strongly with Beria over the German crisis and doubted that he was really a communist, later disclaimed any responsibility for his subsequent fate, saying that was Khrushchev's affair.

After six months' interrogation, Beria was put on trial. The main charges against him, published in *Pravda* on 17 December 1953, were that he planned to seize power and overthrow the Soviet regime, had contacts with foreign intelligence, conducted political intrigues (notably against other Georgians), and was guilty of corruption. So far, so predictable, for those who remembered the show trials of the 1930s. A small paragraph near the end of the announcement noted enigmatically that the investigation had uncovered other crimes 'bearing witness to his deep moral degradation'. The details, mainly second- but some first-hand accounts of Beria preying on young women, subsequently leaked into the rumour mill and left him tainted with a reputation as a sexual predator – which most people probably found more plausible than that he was Trial and execution of Beria a spy. He was found guilty as charged and swiftly executed – a coup accomplished without any public disturbance.

The immediate popular reaction to the news of Beria's

downfall was confusion, with a degree of discredit to the new leadership. 'You can't believe anybody,' people said. There was speculation that Beria was a Jew, perhaps in league with the doctor-murderers (who many thought had been allowed to emigrate to America). New rumours about Stalin's death put Beria in the frame alongside the doctors – for instance that all the guards who were at Stalin's dacha when he died were put on a plane and sent for vacation to a resort, but the plane was blown up on Beria's orders.

Over time, particularly within the Soviet intelligentsia and in the West, Beria's posthumous reputation as a sexual predator confirmed his status as the evil genius of Soviet politics, both under Stalin and after him. This is the underpinning of the story told by Iannucci in his film *The Death of Stalin* (and, before him, by Nury in his graphic novel, *La Mort de Staline*), where Beria's downfall is the denouement that turns the black comedy of Stalin's death into something like a grim morality play, with the villain finally getting his just desserts.

Beria as reformer But Beria, evil though he may have been, was also the main author of the radical reforms introduced on Stalin's death, and continued, albeit in slightly different form, after his own fall. These reforms, initiated by the 'collective leadership' with Beria the main instigator, were later extended by Khrushchev and publicized, under the name of 'Khrushchev's Thaw' – part of the process by which he established himself as the new top dog in the Politburo in 1956. In our story, Beria's death is not the final denouement but rather an anomalous episode – violent but surprisingly minor in its political effects – in the Soviet Union's post-Stalin path towards a more permissive and relaxed regime.

It turned out to be a stroke of brilliance on the part of Beria's associates to remove him, as it then became possible to pile all the blame for Stalinist terror on his shoulders. This included the Great Purges, even though his promotion to the top security job in Moscow post-dated them. As Crankshaw remembered, the 'outburst of singing' in the intelligentsia signalling the first thaw seemed to be a direct response to Beria's arrest, not because he was a 'Stalinist' on cultural questions (he wasn't) but because it implied a repudiation of the terror of the Stalin era. That repudiation, which was clearly one of the main aims of the collective leadership (and of Beria himself), would have been much more difficult to pull off with Stalin's police chief still on the team. As a bonus, any Stalinist policy the new leaders decided to change could now be called Beria's, reducing the risk of public backlash.

Beria as universal scapegoat

As the first anniversary of Stalin's death came round, the collective leadership could breathe a sigh of relief. They had survived not only the transition but also, remarkably, the trial and execution of one of their own members without letting their internal conflicts spill out into the public arena. Apart from some unhappiness in Georgia (where Stalin's death and Beria's disgrace meant a loss of the republic's status within the Union), there had been little pushback and no significant civil disturbances. Important reforms had been set in train, abandoning a good part of Stalin's legacy, even as Stalin's statues kept ponderous watch in Moscow and all the republican capitals, and his embalmed body lay in the Mausoleum next to Lenin's. It was a considerable political feat on the part of Stalin's successors. All the same Stalin, even as a ghost, still had a few tricks up his sleeve.

You Were Always A Great Friend Of Mine, Josep

3/5/1953

CHAPTER FOUR

Reactions Abroad

Ever since 1946, I know that all the so-called experts have been yapping about what would happen when Stalin dies and what we, as a nation, should do about it. Well, he's dead. And you can turn the files of our government inside out – in vain – looking for any plans laid. We have no plan. We are not even sure what difference his death makes.

That was President Dwight Eisenhower's withering summation of United States contingency planning, spoken off the cuff at a meeting of his cabinet two days after Stalin's death. It wasn't that the United States public and political elites were indifferent to Stalin's Soviet Union: they saw it as evil and irredeemably expansionist, a threat to American values and world leadership. Nor did they fail to appreciate Stalin's paramount role within the Soviet political system: if anything, they exaggerated it. The problem was that, up close, they knew almost nothing about the Soviet Union. As a result of that country's effective border control and the paucity of direct contacts with its leaders since the breakup of the wartime alliance, the Western Allies had no good inside sources to give them a sense of the real-life Soviet political scene and what the leaders were thinking. They were guessing, moreover in a context of public hysteria and anti-communist witch-hunting that only made it harder.

US and Soviet stereotypes
The mood of the times is well conveyed in NSC-68, a confidential memo of April 1950 on US security objectives from

Facing page: Herb Block's Pulitzer-winning cartoon on the death of Stalin, published in the *Washington Post* in 1953.

President Truman's National Security Council. This identified the Soviet Union as 'a totalitarian dictatorship' which, 'unlike previous aspirants to hegemony, is animated by a new fanatic faith, antithetical to our own, and seeks to impose its absolute authority over the rest of the world'. Any further expansion of 'the area under the domination of the Kremlin' would involve 'destruction not only of this Republic but of civilization itself'.

Anti-Sovietism was a familiar theme in American politics, but the apocalyptic note was new. The familiar version, as represented by old Russia hands in the US State Department, was characterized by contempt for 'the Bolsheviks', as well as the left-wing American intellectuals who took their socialist claims seriously. But these experts looked like fuddy duddy area specialists to the new generation of political scientists. Led in the US by Harvard's Carl J. Friedrich, they had recently embraced the notion of totalitarianism. Even as Stalin lay dying in March 1953, leading American and European scholars were en route to Cambridge, Massachusetts, to discuss this exciting concept, whose central insight was the innate similarity of Nazi Germany, the wartime enemy, and the Communist Soviet Union, its postwar successor in the enemy role. 'Totalitarianism' was a perfect fit for the Cold War. Indeed, the term had already entered the vocabulary of Congress and the US media with the enunciation of the Truman Doctrine in March 1947, which posited that 'totalitarian regimes ... undermine the foundations of international peace and hence the security of the United States', meaning that the US was bound to oppose them.

Totalitarian regimes, the scholars gathered in Cambridge agreed, had certain defined characteristics. Expansionist and hostile to the democratic West, they were run by dictators who were the object of a Leader cult, at the head of a ruling party, a secret police, and a propaganda machine that 'brainwashed' citizens with a sinister 'ideology' that made them blind to the misery of their situation. It was generally assumed that totalitarian systems, once established, were incapable of reform, and could only collapse as a result of some external event (defeat in war, in the case of Nazi Germany). 'The totalitarian regime does not shed its police-state characteristics,' wrote

Totalitarianism defined

one of the participants, Merle Fainsod, in his classic text published later the same year. 'It dies when power is wrenched from its hands.'

How totalitarian regimes die

The consensus of the March 1953 conference was that nothing on the domestic or international scene looked likely to accomplish that in the near future. But that left unanswered the question of what would happen if, without having power wrenched from his hands, a totalitarian leader simply died. Was it a moment when the whole brittle structure might collapse, perhaps as result of a succession struggle gone out of control due to the absence of institutional processes to ensure a peaceful transition? That would have been a welcome outcome, but the experts were not optimistic. Most thought that the embedded police controls were strong enough to keep the regime afloat even in the case of a contested succession. What almost everyone agreed on was that totalitarian regimes did not change their spots no matter what.

While expansionist ambitions were widely seen as part of Soviet DNA, some of its manifestations were more worrisome than others. First of these was the establishment of pro-Soviet regimes in Eastern Europe, under Soviet pressure, after the Second World War. The Soviets saw these are a necessary buffer against future aggression from the West on the lines of Germany in the Second World War; but from the Western point of view, especially in a context of possible electoral victories for communist parties in France and Italy, it looked like the beginning of a European takeover. Next came the establishment of a Communist regime in China in 1949, dramatically changing the balance of power in Asia. Then in 1951 came the Korean War, which pitted North Korean forces with Soviet and Chinese backing against US- (and ultimately United Nations-) backed South Korean forces. In fact the Soviet Union was a somewhat unwilling partner in this North-Korean-initiated and China-supported enterprise, but this was not how it looked at the time. To Western observers, it was another proof of a Soviet-led communist bid for world domination, all the more dangerous for the fact that Asia was now full of national liberation movements with communist connections looking to take

Fears about Soviet expansion

advantage of the postwar collapse of European empires. And then, of course, there was the atomic bomb, developed and used in 1945 at Hiroshima and Nagasaki by the Americans, which the Soviets had the nerve to copy in 1949, thanks to an effective nuclear programme overseen by Beria. When the Americans went one better with the development of the much more powerful hydrogen bomb in 1952, the Soviets followed close on their heels, successfully testing it (after Stalin's and Beria's demise) in August 1953.

Soviet ideas about capitalists
The Soviets had their own stereotypes about the capitalist West, now led by the United States, and the threat it posed to them. As Nikolai Novikov, ambassador in Washington, cabled on 27 September 1946 'the foreign policy of the United States, which reflects the imperialist tendencies of American monopolistic capital, is characterized in the postwar period by a striving <u>for world supremacy</u> [underlined by Novikov's boss, Foreign Minister Vyacheslav Molotov]... This is the real meaning of the many statements by President Truman and other representatives of American ruling circles: that the United States has the right to lead the world... In the eyes of American imperialists [the Soviet Union] is the main obstacle in the path of the United States to world domination'. All this explained the huge ongoing build-up in military expenditure, which strongly suggested preparation for a third world war, in which the enemy would be the Soviet Union.

In principle Marxist-Leninist theory could have been used to postulate the inevitability of military conflict between the socialist (Soviet-led) and capitalist worlds; and American commentators often assumed that this was indeed the basis of Soviet geopolitical thinking. This wasn't so, partly because of the Soviet leaders' acute consciousness that in the near term they were in no position to wage a successful war against the United States, given the devastation of Soviet economic infrastructure during the Second World War and its huge military and civilian casualties, not to mention that the US currently held the trump card of the atomic bomb. From the Soviet standpoint, Eastern Europe as a buffer was non-negotiable, but that did not mean they planned to turn Western Europe Communist too. China's communists, though allies whose victory was a matter of satisfaction, were not under Moscow's control; and peace in Korea was negotiable.

Stalin met few western leaders in the postwar period, and made few global pronouncements on international affairs. When he did speak, he said that coexistence between the two systems was possible, but there had to be a will to cooperate on both sides; that the current threat of war came not from the Soviets but from the Americans; and that he was open to discussions about how to preserve world peace, including settlement of the Korean War. He also complained that, whenever he said anything about peace, Western diplomats and media dismissed it as a cunning ruse. This last claim was true, but it was also understandable in light of the extremely aggressive and hostile behaviour of Soviet diplomats at the UN and elsewhere, which seemed in itself to demonstrate the impossibility of cooperation.

Stalin's longtime No. 2 Vyacheslav Molotov, in Soviet terms a Cold Warrior, was not a natural diplomat. He had cut his diplomatic teeth negotiating with Ribbentrop and Hitler, whom he hated, over the Nazi-Soviet Pact in 1939, and after the war he used the same dogged and grating approach with Western diplomats, whom he liked no better. Even Archibald Clark Kerr, postwar British Ambassador to the Soviet Union, who could get on with Stalin, drew the line at the 'malevolent' Molotov, whose behaviour abroad was not sweetened by the fact that his political life was on the line and that Stalin had accused him, extraordinarily, of currying favour with the West. According to Anatoly Dobrynin, a future Soviet Ambassador to Washington, it was like 'a dialogue of the deaf and the blind' when Molotov spoke to President Eisenhower's Secretary of State, John Foster Dulles – and this was in 1955, when things had supposedly improved from Stalinist times. The chief Soviet representative at the United Nations, Andrei Vyshinsky, notorious as the State Prosecutor in the Moscow show trials of the 1930s, clashed repeatedly with Foster Dulles and others at the United Nations: for Dulles, his 'arrogant intransigence' illuminated 'the magnitude of the task of saving Europe for Western civilization'.

'A dialogue of the deaf and blind'

Intelligence wars

Where the Soviets clearly excelled, far outstripping the West in the postwar years, was espionage and counterintelligence. With the advantage of information from the 'Cambridge Five' – including Guy Burgess at the Foreign Office in London, Donald Maclean, 1st secretary at British Embassy in Washington, and Kim Philby, heading British intelligence in Istanbul – the Soviets were extremely well supplied with intelligence, not only about British but also American activities and plans. This presumably told them that the US, for all its Cold War huffing and puffing, was not imminently planning a direct nuclear attack on the Kremlin, favouring two alternative strategies, spearheaded by the new US intelligence service, the CIA, rather than the military: stirring up trouble in Eastern Europe, on the one hand, and hurling a propaganda barrage at the Soviet population, on the other. The Soviet Union was all too aware of the West's efforts to organize a 'fifth column' within the communist bloc, and the anti-cosmopolitan campaign of Stalin's last years was surely in part a response to it.

Western intelligence on the Soviet Union was at a very low ebb in the years between the end of the war and Stalin's death: in this respect, 'the West picked itself off the floor in 1945,' a senior British intelligence official remembered, and was still on its knees in the late forties. It was no better in the US, where 'intelligence files on the Soviet Union were virtually empty', lacking even basic information on roads, bridges, airfields, the location of factories or city maps. The West had no highly placed sources in Moscow and scarcely any agents except in Berlin – certainly nothing to match the 'steady flow of Soviet spies to the West'. Moscow was undoubtedly pleased with its intelligence superiority, but looked at objectively, more inside knowledge of the Soviet Union on the West's part might have served Soviet interests better. As it was, 'no one questioned the capacity of the Russians to carry out their Grand Design to rule the world' – an analysis failure that CIA Russia specialist Harry Rositzke described as 'at least partly due to a failure of intelligence'.

That was the setting for the inadequate US response to Stalin's death that Eisenhower noted. After Stalin, died, the new

Uneven
intelligence

leaders – notably Malenkov, in his 'peace' speech at Stalin's funeral – did their best to send out a message to the West that the new regime was willing to deal, but it was largely ignored. Western intelligence experts and politicians were used to dismissing Soviet 'peace' talk: the line was that '"friendly" Soviet moves were described as "lures", while unfriendly moves were said to reveal the true Soviet intentions'. On this occasion, too, the experts dismissed any changes in Soviet foreign policy as 'purely tactical, short-term, and designed to make the regime more popular'. When, a month after the funeral, *Pravda* published a concrete Soviet overture (willingness to talk about the problem of Germany's division), MI6 allegedly did not know who Malenkov was.

Overtures ignored

Failures of Western intelligence were exacerbated by the fact that the United States was in the throes of its own regime change, albeit via the regular and routinized process of presidential elections. Republican Dwight Eisenhower became President in December 1952, succeeding Democrat Harry Truman, and was inaugurated on 20 January 1953, just six weeks before Stalin's death. Eisenhower, former commander of Allied forces in Europe, had no personal stake in keeping the Soviets at arm's length, but toughness on Communism had been a big issue in the campaign. The Republicans had lambasted Truman's administration for its defensive policy of 'containment' and proposed an alternative strategy aimed at inspiring revolt in Communist countries and 'rolling back' communism. All the while, Senator Eugene McCarthy's House of Un-American Activities Committee was busy unmasking domestic Communists, with suspicion falling even on Eisenhower's nominee for the vacant post of Ambassador to the Soviet Union, the respected State Department Russia expert Charles Bohlen.

Eisenhower and John Foster Dulles

Responding to the mood of the moment, Eisenhower said at his inaugural in January that 'forces or good and evil are massed and armed and opposed as rarely before in history. Freedom is pitted against slavery, lightness against the dark'. He appointed one of the most virulent anti-Communists on

65

the US political scene, John Foster Dulles, as his Secretary of State. Foster Dulles, as a Christian and a capitalist, had always hated Bolshevism. But with its rise to superpower status, he saw it almost in apocalyptic terms – not just 'a challenge to established civilization' but 'the kind of thing which occurs only once in centuries', comparable with 'the challenge of Islam to Christianity in the tenth century'. He disliked it much more than he had ever disliked Nazism, though this is not to make a huge claim. In an article published in *Life* magazine in 1952 which became the Republicans' foreign policy mantra in the Presidential campaign, he advocated 'a policy of boldness' towards the Soviet Union involving 'massive retaliation' in the event of any expansion of its geographical reach.

Stalin, Hitler, Bismarck, Attila and Nero: enemies of God and of the USA. Secretary of State Dulles would likely have sympathised with the message of this cartoon, published in the *Catholic Times* in March 1953.

This was the big vision; the nitty-gritty of responding to Stalin's death was another matter altogether. Both Foster Dulles and his brother Allen, who headed the CIA, favoured undermining the Soviet Union by making trouble in the satellites and destabilizing Soviet clients rather than by head-on confrontation with Moscow. Indeed, on the day before Stalin's death, the National Security Council had met to discuss plans to overthrow an alleged Soviet puppet in Iran, Mohammad Mosaddegh, an issue that remained an intense preoccupation with both the Americans and the British until his eventual removal in August.

With such excitement in progress, it was hard to focus on the Soviet Union, despite its logical priority. Should the United States make some kind of public statement on Stalin's death? The State Department counselled 'salutary silence until we had collected our facts, along with our wits'. In the ensuing discussion, some thought Stalin's death was the perfect opportunity for an 'aggressive response', while others worried this might seem crass – it was a 'family funeral' for the Soviets, after all, Foster Dulles noted, and better to wait on any bold initiative until 'the corpse was buried and the mourners gone off to their homes to read the will'. Dulles, for all his belligerent stance towards the Soviet Union, had no thoughts of direct military action, still less a pre-emptive nuclear strike; and neither option would have been countenanced by Eisenhower, whose experience as a military man had led him to regard war as the worst possible outcome. What Dulles had in mind was something combining stepped-up covert action in the bloc with a propaganda offensive – 'winning World War III without having to fight it'.

Perhaps without Foster Dulles at his side, Eisenhower would have been more open to overtures from the new Soviet leaders; on the other hand, Foster Dulles was his appointee, and he knew what he was getting. When Eisenhower asked Dulles if Malenkov's funeral speech did not suggest that the new Soviet leaders were interested in negotiating a way out of Cold War (as well as out of the hot war in Korea), he was assured that it did not: these were just smoke signals intended to confuse the West. Eisenhower was not wholly convinced; a

Act now or wait and see?

part of him wanted to be the president of peace, calling a halt to the international arms race, and he saw Stalin's death as a possible opportunity for a reset. After his friend and counsellor Emmett Hughes visited Moscow early in 1954, he told Eisenhower confidentially that 'If the Soviet Union is politically and psychologically geared for major aggressive war, then we're living in the sixteenth century and I'm Martin Luther' – to which Eisenhower replied: 'I have long been in agreement.' It was these instincts that led him to make his famous 'Chance for Peace' speech on 16 April 1953, suggesting that he was an open to overtures from the Soviet Union while implying that it was up to the new leaders – who now had 'a precious opportunity... to help turn the tide of history' – to take the initiative. Whether they would rise to this opportunity was still unclear, but the Americans would 'welcome every honest act of peace'. Specifically, the United States stood ready to proceed with 'the next great work' – discussion under United Nations auspices on disarmament and arms limitation.

Eisenhower as president of peace

Support for seizing the 'chance for peace' presented by Stalin's death now came from an unexpected source – British Tory Prime Minister Winston Churchill, back in office in October 1951, after being voted out in July 1945. Churchill had a long and contradictory history with the Soviet Union, starting as a passionate supporter of the anti-Bolshevik Whites in the Russian Civil War of 1918–20, but becoming part of the remarkably successful, even friendly, Allied triumvirate of Roosevelt, Churchill and Stalin during the Second World War. In 1946, Churchill had been the man to point out that Europe was now divided by an 'Iron Curtain' separating East and West, a key text in the formulation of Cold War. But in 1953, instinctively recognizing that Stalin's death created possibilities of change, Churchill did his best to punch some holes in that same Iron Curtain. Experts remained sceptical, however, and Britain was no longer in a position to take the lead. It was in vain that throughout 1953, Churchill pushed the Americans to agree to summit talks with the new Soviet leaders.

Eisenhower's 'Chance for Peace' initiative foundered, as a result of Eisenhower's own lethargy in pursuing it and Foster Dulles's vigilance in impeding it. At the first Cabinet meeting after his speech, Eisenhower was absent playing golf in Atlanta, and the implications of what he had said were not even discussed. The Soviets published the text in full in *Pravda* – an extremely positive signal – while criticizing its failure to offer specifics and US encouragement of dissent in Eastern Europe. CIA head Allen Dulles noticed this, along with a series of follow-up gestures from Malenkov, with some surprise (the standard line was that Malenkov was likely one the most orthodox Stalinists in a succession regime, whereas Molotov might be open to new ideas). US Sovietologists continued to get Malenkov wrong, advising after he became head of the Soviet government that his aim would be to establish a personal dictatorship and that meanwhile he would 'play a cautious game' in foreign policy. In fact, as Eisenhower noted in his memoirs, 'far earlier than anyone had expected, he launched a peace offensive' whose 'apparent purpose [was] to avoid a global war... and slow up the rearmament of the United States and the West' – which, as it happened, was what Eisenhower wanted too.

The scene might have been set for a steady movement towards détente twenty years earlier than this actually occurred. But on the American side, the public had embraced the demonization of communism and the notion of Soviet expansionism to the point that it was simply not ready for détente. The other problem was that the Dulles brothers, who had a very strong hold on US policy-making, neither believed that there was a real chance for peace nor, it seemed, wanted it. Foster Dulles was against talk of disarmament, and both brothers doubted the utility of the four-power summit urged by, among others, Churchill. Their focus was on a quite different approach to the Soviet Union: 'psychological warfare'.

Run out of a special Office of Policy Coordination, at first nominally separate but later a part of the CIA's Clandestine Services Department, psychological warfare included 'dirty tricks', such as the plan, hatched before Stalin's death but apparently never put into action, to 'maximise confusion' in the Soviet Union by spreading rumours that he was not really dead and that corrupt high officials had fled the country with their ill-gotten gains. Disinformation campaigns, whose

Psychological warfare

purpose was to undermine trust in the Soviet Union, were launched in Communist states such as China and Yugoslavia. To encourage defections from the Soviet bloc, defectors were lionized as heroes who had chosen freedom over Communist oppression.

'Liberation' propaganda, aimed primarily at the 'captive nations' of Eastern Europe rather than the Soviet Union itself, was another keystone. 'It is only by keeping alive the hope of liberation, by taking advantage of that wherever opportunity arises, that we will end this terrible peril which dominates the world,' Foster Dulles told the Senate Foreign Relations Committee at his confirmation as Secretary of State. 'Keeping the hope alive', it turned out, meant encouraging Eastern European to rebel, but not (as Hungarian 'freedom-fighters' found to their cost in 1956) offering concrete military assistance if they did so. The point – as outlined in the secret NSC directive 158 (29 June 1953) – was to fan whatever discontent existed so as to 'undermine the authority of the satellite governments' and then 'make propaganda use of East European unrest as a sign that the Soviet empire was crumbling'.

The voice of J. Roksanov, a Russian announcer employed by the Voice of America (*Golos Ameriki*), is beamed from Washington to the Soviet Union in December 1954.

A further ongoing cause of Soviet irritation was the issue of Soviet 'displaced persons' (DPs) – wartime forced labourers and prisoners of war left in Germany and Austria after the war, whose repatriation was demanded by the Soviets, but resisted by the DPs themselves. In the face of bad press back home, the Western Allies soon stopped cooperating on Soviet repatriation, resulting in what the Soviet Union regarded as the 'theft' of half a million Soviet citizens. This was bad enough, but even worse was that the Americans were financing anti-Soviet organizations among the DPs, going so far as to provide the aircraft to drop agents (small numbers, quickly detected) into Soviet territory. There was even an almost successful push in 1952 to form a Volunteer Freedom Corps of European DPs to serve under American command, presumably to be used in the event of war with the Soviet Union.

Among the advantages of the US emphasis on covert action and psychological warfare were that the costs were low and military action was not involved, both characteristics that appealed to President Eisenhower. At the same time the approach worked against Eisenhower's stated desire for rapprochement with the Soviet leaders over disarmament. Psychological warfare was calculated to annoy as well as to undermine Soviet leaders, and it is clear that in the former aim, it succeeded. The last thing it was likely to promote was the trust necessary to begin negotiation.

Pros and cons of psychological warfare

If the US did little to further rapprochement with the Soviet Union after Stalin's death, the Soviet effort was also lukewarm: in foreign policy, the new leaders' reform impulse was nowhere near as strong and consistent as it was in domestic. In the first place, foreign policy was the purview of Molotov (as it had been for many years under Stalin), and Molotov's attitude to the West was as suspicious as Stalin's. Malenkov, Beria and Khrushchev all wanted a more determined effort at rapprochement, but their efforts were stymied, first by the uprising of June 1953 in Berlin and, a few weeks later, by the ousting of Beria. To be sure, they did move fairly swiftly to end the Korean War (the armistice was announced on 27 July 1953). But in the view of Anatoly Dobrynin, later pioneer of a new style of Soviet diplomacy and proponent of détente, 'they did not venture beyond the minimal steps necessary to avoid direct conflicts with the United States and to project an image of themselves as strong, but more peaceful than Stalin'. With John Foster Dulles as Secretary of State, it is not surprising that, whatever their desire for change, the new Soviet leaders might have felt they could do little to change relations with the United States, whose superpower primacy, confidence and wealth in any case overawed them. Georgi Arbatov, longtime head of the Soviet Institute for the study of the USA, considered that 'the situation was such that any initiative, even a purely symbolic one, had to come from the West, and especially from the United States' – and it didn't come.

The death of Stalin was undoubtedly a potential turning point in East-West relations. But – as A. J. P. Taylor said of Europe's 1848 revolutions – it was a turning point that failed to turn. Not until 1956, with Khrushchev's partial denunciation of Stalin (which the CIA did its part in publicizing), did the West finally recognize that a significant thaw was in process within the Soviet Union. But widespread resistance remained to the idea that the Soviet regime could actually move away from totalitarianism without being forced to by external pressure. Real efforts towards détente had to wait more than another decade, and even then were undermined by residual Cold War sentiments and fears: it was as late as 1983 that US President Ronald Reagan famously characterized the Soviet Union as 'the evil empire'. The Cold War ended only with the Soviet Union's dissolution in 1991, almost forty years after Stalin's death.

Missed opportunity?

CHAPTER 5

Stalin's Ghost

Stalin's new grave after his body was removed from the Mausoleum in the early 1960s.

'I know that after my death they will throw a bunch of rubbish on my grave,' Molotov remembered Stalin saying during the war. 'But the wind of history will mercilessly blow it away.' Stalin was certainly right about the bunch of rubbish, but which way the winds would blow was another matter.

In the first years after Stalin's death, his legacy, particularly the terror of the 1930s, was the great unmentionable. His body lay next to Lenin's in the Mausoleum, and his statues still stood in prominent positions throughout the land. But his name had abruptly disappeared from the media after his death, with no explanation offered. Many of the policies associated with his rule had been dropped, similarly without explicit repudiation. In the process of Beria's removal in mid 1953, the blame for various 'mistakes' and 'abuses' of the Stalin years had been laid at his security chief's door – an acknowledgement that they had occurred but one that left Stalin's part unexamined. While it was convenient for Stalin's successors to have Beria as a scapegoat, the line didn't fully take with the Soviet public, who tended to be distracted by red herrings like whether Beria had been in league with the Jewish doctors. As for the savvy 'fraternal' Communists running Eastern European countries, they simply scoffed at the idea that Beria was Stalin's evil genius. When Khrushchev tried this line on the Yugoslavs, they told him 'in plain, simple language ... "Stalin was the principal killer"'; and Khrushchev had to admit that this was the case.

Khrushchev had his own reasons for thinking about Stalin's legacy. Ambitious for the top job, he undoubtedly had an eye for things that would damage Politburo colleagues who were potential opponents, and the negative 'Stalin card' was one of them. Molotov had been Stalin's principal associate since the 1920s, while Malenkov had been his right-hand man on questions of party organization and appointments for more than a decade. Khrushchev, by contrast, had joined the Politburo only in 1939 and since then had worked primarily in Ukraine, that is, outside Moscow and not in daily contact with Stalin. In any mud-slinging contest about sharing responsibility with Stalin for past wrongs, he was likely to come out the winner.

Playing the 'Stalin card'

Another factor bringing the issue of Stalin's legacy into political play was the return from Gulag of rehabilitated 'politicals', mainly victims of the Great Purges. A Rehabilitation Commission under Politburo member Anastas Mikoyan had been set up to consider individual petitions, and was steadily approving them. Many of the rehabilitated, from Molotov's wife on down, were Communists personally known to members of the leadership. As they straggled back, turning to their old friends in an effort to recover lost housing and jobs in Moscow, they related harrowing stories of fifteen years in Gulag. These stories genuinely to have shaken the new leaders, particularly Mikoyan and Khrushchev. Activist returnees whom they respected lobbied them intensively for a public confrontation with the issue of Stalinist terror.

Denunciation of Stalin cult, 1956

For its own better information on the Great Purges and their consequences, the Politburo commissioned a secret investigation by Petr Pospelov, a senior Communist official. Pospelov was not known as a reformer, which made his findings, presented to the Politburo on the eve of the Twentieth Party Congress in February 1956, all the more explosive. In the Great Purges, he reported that, on the basis of secret police data, close to 2 million people were arrested for anti-Soviet activities, and almost 700,000 of them summarily shot. 'What kind of leader is it, if he destroys everybody,' was the first line of the confidential summary of the Politburo meeting discussing the report on 9 February 1956 (evidently the rapporteur was too upset to find the proper formal language). The Politburo members agreed that they 'had to have the courage to tell the truth' to the party, admitting the existence of 'a cult of personality, the concentration of power in one person's hands. In impure hands'. Even Molotov agreed, though he thought the Party should also be reminded of Stalin's achievements as an industrializer and nation-builder.

Granted that they were going to tell 'the truth', which truth was that exactly? Was it only Stalin's sins against the party that mattered, or should wartime errors of judgement also be discussed? How about collectivization? That stood out in popular memory as the quintessential episode of terror in the Stalin period, but the victims were peasants, with party members as perpetrators. The Politburo members did not immediately address these questions, being preoccupied by issues of specifically party-factional interest (was Stalin right to destroy the Trotskyists?), and with the general suspicion that Molotov, Kaganovich and Voroshilov, even though they agreed to vote with the consensus, had private reservations.

On the last day of the Congress in Moscow, Khrushchev seized the ball with his 'Secret Speech' to Congress delegates. Stalin's 'cult of personality', a euphemism for personal dictatorship, was the central charge. The real issue, however, was not dictatorship but terror, and what really rocked the delegates was detailed information on the Great Purges and their impact on the Communist party elite. The fact that 70 per cent of Central Committee members and alternates elected at the 1934 Party Congress were arrested and shot before the next Congress came around in 1939 elicited gasps from the delegates. They were shocked to learn that, had Stalin lived

Khrushchev's 'Secret Speech'

75

a few months longer, Molotov and Mikoyan would probably not have been around to deliver speeches at the present Congress. The Doctors' Plot, more familiar ground, was debunked again ('fabricated from beginning to end,' Khrushchev told the Congress). Going beyond Pospelov's report, Khrushchev offered his own sensational speculation that Stalin might have been behind the 1934 murder of Politburo member Sergei Kirov, and called for an investigation (subsequent exhaustive searches of the archives produced no proof).

There was much less in Khrushchev's speech about crimes or policy errors in which elite Party members were likely to have been complicit. Collectivization was not criticized as such, although Khrushchev faulted Stalin for ignoring the poor performance of Soviet agriculture and caring nothing for the welfare of the peasantry. It would probably have been politic on Khrushchev's part to stay away from the Second World War, which ended in a much-celebrated victory under Stalin's leadership, but, as so often happened, he got carried away on hobby horses of his own about Stalin's wartime leadership, debunking Stalin's vaunted military expertise. The Congress's brief resolution on Khrushchev's speech stopped short of the direct repudiation of Stalinist terror that it seemed to call for, instead focussing on Stalin's 'cult of personality', a term never satisfactorily defined. The resolution promised measures that would get rid of the 'consequences' of the cult in all walks of life – a vague assurance, concretised only in its affirmation of 'the principles of collective leadership worked out by the great Lenin', that is, rule by the Politburo.

But that was only the beginning. News of the speech, initially intended for delegates' ears alone, flew around the country (indeed, thanks to the CIA, around the world); and it was subsequently read out, though not published, in meetings at workplaces throughout the Soviet Union, among them one in the Moscow Institute of Literature where Stalin's daughter Svetlana was a researcher. She listened in stunned silence, and at the end, when a colleague helped her on with her coat, burst into tears at this act of kindness: the colleague was Andrei Sinyavsky, author of the 'howling dog' passage on Stalin's death quoted in chapter 3. The intense national discussion that followed the speech, a precursor to that of Gorbachev's glasnost in the late 1980s, elicited passionate attacks on and defence of many different aspects of Stalin's legacy, which in effect meant the whole political and social structure of the Soviet Union. Original uncorrupted 'Leninism' was invoked as the opposite of 'Stalinism', sometimes sincerely, by Communists such as Roy Medvedev, and sometimes as a tactic to legitimate reform proposals. It was not yet a dissident conversation (that would come later) but rather one of those rare moments when societies are moved by the sense that fundamental change is possible, and individuals feel they can be part of the process. Young people, in particular, responded idealistically to the cause of reform – building socialism still, but a better version than the Stalinist one.

Writers embraced the cultural Thaw, and huge reputations were made by those using the new freedom of expression. Charismatic young poets such as Yevgeny Yevtushenko filled football stadiums passionately reciting their 'truth-telling' work. The journal *Novy Mir* (to which Tvardovsky returned as editor) spearheaded the cultural renovation movement. Its lobbying persuaded Khrushchev to override the censor and publish Alexander Solzhenitsyn's first novella, *One Day in the Life of Ivan Denisovich*, describing a prisoner's life in Gulag (which, as a former *zek* himself, he knew at first hand). The literary discussion, for the most part, focussed not on Stalin

'Truth-telling'

personally, but on the need for social, political and cultural change and moral regeneration in the Soviet Union. For example, Vladimir Dudintsev's *Not by Bread Alone*, one of the iconic works of Thaw literature, has nothing to say directly about Stalin but is all about soulless bureaucrats impeding innovation.

The reactions of ordinary people to the Twentieth Party Congress varied. Many who had been brought up venerating Stalin 'simply could not believe that such things could be true', as Mikhail Gorbachev, then a party official in Stavropol, remembered. He himself was not among them: he knew about terror, since members of his own family had fallen victim. He was surprised, however, by some negative reactions to de-stalinization among local peasants, who remembered 1937 in positive terms as the time when Stalin purged their oppressors, the local bosses. In the Volga town of Molotovo (known as Perm until 1940), abuses by local bosses – swearing at their subordinates, exploiting the workers and allowing their wives to swan around in official cars eating pastries – were also part of the discussion. But there they were invoked by de-stalinizers, as a part of the 'cult of personality' of their own 'little Stalins'. Many of the grievances vented in the discussion of the 'cult of personality' were local and particular, directed against whatever official policies and practices had caused most annoyance. In Moscow's Gnesin School of Music, students interpreted de-stalinization as meaning that they should have access to Stravinsky and other 'formalist' music denounced in the Zhdanov campaign of the late 1940s.

There was muttering among party office-holders about Stalin's dethronement, but it was only in Georgia that there were significant riots or outbreaks of public protest. Despite Stalin's personal lack of Georgian nationalism and his identification with Russia, Georgia had done well in the Stalin period. Its peasantry had suffered comparatively little in collectivization, thanks in part to Beria's protection, and it was one of only two non-Russian republics that had mostly been run by party bosses of the local nationality (the other was Armenia). Beria's fall had been a blow to the republics' political elite, since, in a system in which patron-client relations

The statue
of Stalin in
Tbilisi, site of
anti-Russian
protests in
1956.

played a key role, he had been Georgia's patron-in-chief in
Moscow since the late 1930s. The Georgians' adverse reaction
to Khrushchev's Secret Speech was a direct response to its den-
igration of Stalin, a native son. Khrushchev – a leader whose
own ties were with Ukraine – had allowed himself a rash
reference to "'the great son of the Georgian nation", as Georgians liked to refer to Stalin', which was taken as an insult to
all Georgians. The offence was exacerbated by Khrushchev's

lengthy rehearsal of old attacks on Beria, whose fall at the end of 1953 had been followed by a painful purging of Beria's numerous clients within the Georgian political elite.

In the wake of the speech, there were popular disturbances in Tbilisi, which quickly turned nationalist and anti-Russian. The Georgian party boss Vasil Mzhavanadze promised to defend Stalin's name and allow celebrations of his achievements in the press, as well as mourning meetings to be held in his honour. But this was not enough to calm the situation. Rumours spread that Chinese Communist leader Mao Tse Tung, known to be unhappy with the Soviet denunciation of Stalin, would visit Tbilisi to make the protest movement international, and that Stalin's children, Vasily and Svetlana, were on their way as well, to make it dynastic. Leaflets calling for Georgian independence started to circulate. On the night of 9 March, Moscow sent in the army to quell the street disturbances in Tbilisi, but the crowds only grew larger. Shots were fired, killing twenty-two, and hundreds were arrested. Order was restored, but at a cost. The link between Georgian and Soviet patriotism effected under Stalin was damaged and a Georgian nationalism that involved independence from the Soviet Union was reborn.

The impact of the Twentieth Congress was also dramatically manifest in Eastern Europe, where all the satellite regimes had problems of legitimacy because of their dependence on Moscow. In Poland and Hungary, the example of the Soviet Thaw encouraged local Communist parties to remove unpopular 'Stalinist' leaders and put in Communists with a reform agenda. The hope was that Moscow would accept this, and indeed the leaders in the Kremlin agonized about the issue. In the end, however, they decided that the danger of a coup taking these countries out of the Soviet bloc was too great to permit inaction, particularly in light of the United States' commitment to liberation of the 'captive nations'. Soviet tanks were sent in to put down what was classified as rebellion in Hungary, and Communist reformer Imre Nagy was removed as leader and later executed. While the expected CIA help did not materialize, the abortive Hungarian revolution was an important Cold War moment that reverberated throughout the world and sent hundreds of thousands of anti-Communist 'freedom fighters' into exile in the West.

A statue of Stalin is torn down in Budapest during the Hungarian uprising of 1956.

Cracks in the collective leadership

The 'collective leadership' had stayed together, despite internal tensions, for four years. But relations deteriorated in the wake of Beria's ousting, as Khrushchev increasingly thrust himself forward. Pushing Malenkov into the background, he clashed ever more often with Molotov, the member of the leadership most loyal to Stalin and the least enthusiastic about change. Khrushchev's over-the-top performance at the Twentieth Party Congress dispersed 'the last remnants of former humility' (as Kaganovich commented disapprovingly) without convincing his old colleagues that he was their natural leader. They increasingly saw him as a loose cannon, particularly when drunk, whose uncensored, off-message utterances were an embarrassment.

Like Beria before them, Khrushchev's colleagues underestimated his political skills and resourcefulness. A majority of the Politburo, led by Molotov, was plotting to discipline him, perhaps even to remove him from the position of party secretary, when Khrushchev, using his powers as head of the party apparat, and with the aid of his ally Mikoyan, struck first, summoning an urgent meeting of the party Central Committee to resolve 'Politburo disagreements'. This was a new tactic in Soviet politics, but it worked. In the resulting week of accusation and counteraccusation, the plotters – Molotov, Malenkov, Voroshilov, Kaganovich and Bulganin – found themselves painted as accomplices or even instigators of Stalin's crimes. As 'the second man after Stalin', Khrushchev told Molotov in an angry exchange, 'you bear the chief responsibility'.

Molotov defended himself vigorously, framing the Politburo conflict as the result of Khrushchev's violations of the principle of collective leadership, and reiterating his claim that, despite mistakes, Stalin had built socialism and strengthened the Soviet Union. The Soviet people, he said, would not support any attempt to deny this. Kaganovich was humbler, admitting that the dethroning of Stalin had caused him suffering and internal struggle. The upshot was that the plotters against Khrushchev were labelled an 'anti-Party group' (an insult that deeply rankled with these dyed-in-the-wool party loyalists), and Molotov, Kaganovich and Malenkov were ejected from the leadership in June 1957. In contrast to Stalinist practice, they were not killed or even arrested, but given lower positions outside the capitals. Kaganovich and Malenkov were sent out to the boondocks to run respectively a chemical factory in the Urals and a hydroelectric plant in Kazakhstan, while Molotov got the ambassadorship to Mongolia. The city of Molotovo resumed its earlier name of Perm, in token of his fall.

Politburo purges

There were four members of the old Stalin team left in the Politburo: Khrushchev, Mikoyan, Voroshilov and Bulganin. But only the first two remained significant political players; the Stalinist old guard was in process of leaving the political stage. Eight new members, all Khrushchev supporters, were elected to an expanded Politburo. One of the new faces was Leonid Brezhnev, a Russian brought into Moscow earlier in the year from his previous job as party secretary in Kazakhstan, who had been an important ally of Khrushchev within the Central Committee in the fight with the old guard.

But Stalin, or his ghost, had not left the political stage. At the Twenty-Second Party Congress in 1961, Khrushchev and his supporters laid into Molotov and the rest as accomplices in Stalin's crimes; one speaker called them 'swamp creatures grown used to slime and dirt'. They were now expelled from the party, in addition to being forced into involuntary retirement (but still at liberty). As for Stalin, a real 'bunch of rubbish' did indeed descend on his reputation, above all as the killer of the Great Purge victims, to whom Khrushchev suggested a monument should be erected in Moscow. Emotions mounted as the Congress proceeded, and on the last day an unscheduled motion was made to have Stalin's body removed from the Mausoleum. The proposal was supported by Dora Lazurkina, an Old Bolshevik now close to eighty who had served a long sentence in Gulag. Egged on by rising applause and a supportive interjection from Khrushchev, she confided to the Congress that 'yesterday I consulted with Ilyich [Lenin], who stood before me as if alive and said: it is unpleasant for me to be next to Stalin, who brought so much trouble on the party'.

'Lazurkina's dream', as this intervention was dubbed, would later be much mocked; and in general Soviet joke-tellers had a field day with this latest development (Lenin's involuntary cohabitation with Stalin in the Mausoleum was often represented, in a snide reference to the perpetual Moscow housing shortage, as a squabble of neighbours in a communal apartment). But the advice of Lenin's ghost was taken, and Stalin's embalmed body was removed from the Mausoleum that same night. The coffin, covered with cement, was reburied behind the Mausoleum near the Kremlin wall. In other cities, statues of Stalin were taken down (a crowd came out to protest in Stavropol, but the statue was removed anyway), and streets named in honour of Stalin were renamed. In Central Asia, Mount Stalin became Mount Communism. Even the city of Stalingrad, famed as the site of the wartime turning point in January 1943, went back to being Volgograd, despite considerable local unhappiness at the change; confusingly, the Battle of Stalingrad kept its old name.

But perhaps even this was not enough to exorcise Stalin's ghost? *Pravda* published an impassioned poem by Yevtushenko, 'The Heirs of Stalin', expressing his fears that Stalin, although now removed from the Mausoleum and buried near the Kremlin Wall, was only 'feigning death', just as some of his heirs (unnamed in the poem) were only feigning to repudiate him:

Lazurkina's dream

I appeal to our government with the request
To double, triple the guards at that wall
So that Stalin will not rise again, and with him the past...

'Stalinists' and 'liberals'

In 1964, in the wake of the Cuban Missile Crisis, Khrushchev got his come-uppance from a Politburo whose members retained a commitment to collective leadership. He was ousted in a Politburo action led by Brezhnev, a more collegial and predictable figure. Western attitudes to Khrushchev were mixed, but there was a consensus that with his partial repudiation of Stalin's legacy he had done the Soviet Union a great service. When Hedrick Smith was sent to Moscow as *New York Times* correspondent, he was surprised to find out that a lot of ordinary Russians saw things differently. 'It came to me as a discovery,' he wrote, 'that Stalin had great latent prestige among ordinary people and that Khrushchev was widely regarded as a boor and a bungler practically without redeeming attributes, except among the liberal intelligentsia and the rehabilitated victims of the purges who had been direct beneficiaries of his policies'. Stalin, people told him, had been a strong boss who had built up the country, won the war and the respect of the world, instilled order and cracked down on bureaucratic corruption. Khrushchev, by contrast, was a buffoon. 'The present leadership has no sense of decorum,' a thirty-year-old woman in Tashkent said. 'When [Stalin] was alive, other countries respected and feared us more.'

'No sense of decorum'

Stalin was not directly an issue in Khruschchev's fall, but after the event many in the West and the Soviet intelligentsia feared a reversal of de-stalinization. In fact, Brezhnev's desire was to contain rather than reverse the process, and his preference was that the issue not be brought up at all, given its sensitivity within the party. But the Politburo he headed (initially first among equals, in the Leninist manner) was prepared to push back against the 'liberal' intelligentsia's interpretation of the Thaw, which included the relaxation of censorship and a continuation of the intense debates of the Khrushchev period on Soviet society and the Stalinist legacy.

This tougher line was manifest in the trial of writers

Andrei Sinyavsky and Yuri Daniel in February 1966 for unauthorized publication abroad of satirical works about the Soviet Union, including Sinyavsky's *The Trial Begins*. When the two received Gulag sentences of seven and five years respectively, a collective shudder went through the intelligentsia. Panicky rumours circulated that the upcoming Twenty-Third Party Congress, the first to be held under Brezhnev's leadership, would see Stalin fully rehabilitated, and a petition signed by cultural and scientific luminaries from the literary and film worlds was sent to Brezhnev urging him against this course. In the event, no such rehabilitation was attempted at the Congress, nor does one seem to have been planned.

An episode taking the story back into the realm of black comedy was the sensational defection of Stalin's daughter Svetlana in 1967. This happened in India, where Svetlana (who after Stalin's death had taken her mother's last name, Alliluyeva) caused a worldwide sensation by impulsively seeking the protection of the US Embassy in Delhi. One of the reasons she cited for her defection was the trial of her friend and sometime lover, Sinyavsky. But the broader context was that she found her life in Moscow – where nobody could ever forget that she was Stalin's daughter – intolerable, and her many love affairs kept going wrong. Privately, her Politburo 'uncles' were surprisingly understanding. But her defection was a Cold War propaganda triumph for the United States at the time, even though her *re*-defection to the Soviet Union in 1984, well-publicized by the other side, later took some of the gloss off. (When she changed her mind for a third time and left the Soviet Union two years later, propagandists on both sides gave up.)

Svetlana's 1967 defection made people think again of Stalin, this time perhaps more as a person than a political figure. The poet Alexander Tvardovsky, *Novy Mir*'s editor, who still kept a portrait of Stalin in his study at the dacha despite being one of the leading critics of Stalinism, was moved to remember the much-quoted words with which Stalin had let him and other children of 'class enemies' off the hook in the mid 1930s: 'a son does not answer for his father'. But should a father be held answerable for his son (in Vasily Stalin's case, a drunken wreck) or his daughter (a defector)? As he tried out variants of a verse on these lines in his diary, Tvardovsky noted that there should be a hint of pity for Stalin, if only as a father.

Relations between Brezhnev and the intelligentsia deteriorated further in 1968 after the Soviet invasion of Czechoslovakia. This replay of Hungary 1956 overthrew Alexander Dubcek's reformist Communist government (one of whose members was, as it happened, Gorbachev's old friend Zdenek Mlynar), which had to all appearances given less provocation than Nagy's twelve years earlier. The invasion was accompanied by a formal announcement (the 'Brezhnev doctrine') of what was already established *de facto*: that any Soviet bloc country that looked like defecting to the West would suffer the same fate. In the wake of the invasion, many Soviet writers signed petitions in protest, but then found themselves on a blacklist, their work unpublishable.

Brezhnev doctrine

The feared rehabilitation of Stalin never happened, even though the estrangement of the regime and reform-minded intelligentsia deepened. The Brezhnev Politburo, mindful that Stalin remained a hero to many Communists, was willing to show a greater degree of respect for him than Khrushchev had done. But this never progressed beyond minor symbolic gestures. When Stalin's body was reburied under the Kremlin Wall in 1961, the spot had been marked only by a bare name and dates. Ten years later, a pedestal appeared, topped by a bust of Stalin by the sculptor Nikolai Tomsky. The Kremlin Wall was in fact, a respectable last resting place for Soviet luminaries. Sergei Kirov and other old Politburo colleagues of Stalin's were buried there, and Brezhnev himself would join them in due course. (Khrushchev, dying in 1971, was rejected for burial in the Kremlin Wall, and had to make do with Moscow's elite Novodevichy Cemetery, where he joined Stalin's wife and Svetlana's mother, Nadezhda Alliluyeva.)

Stalin's ghost continued to haunt the Soviet Union. When Svetlana talked with the head of the Georgian Orthodox Church about her father's death, he told her that 'he had contacts with Stalin's soul in his dreams'. Many people dreamt about Stalin, often recording their dreams in diaries and memoirs. As 'liberals' were more prone than 'Stalinists' to keep diaries or write memoirs, these were often dreams about terror. Alexander Solzhenitsyn, on his way from Gulag incarceration to a sensational literary career as a truth-teller about Stalin's crimes, wrote an autobiographical novel that introduced Stalin as a character: an old, sick, pathologically suspicious man conducting an internal monologue on his past achievements. In the 1970s, small groups of Soviet dissidents, scorning official Soviet holidays and intent on forcing Brezhnev's regime to observe its own laws, gathered every year on 5 March, the anniversary of Stalin's death, and 5 December, the day of promulgation of the Stalin Constitution. The theme of Stalin's resurrection, raised back in the 1960s by Yevtushenko, was repeated in a hit movie coming out of Georgia in the Gorbachev reform years, Tengis Abuladze's *Repentance* (1986), where a Stalin-like local dictator is duly buried, but keeps being dug up by those who think he was a criminal who doesn't deserve a decent grave, and then reburied by his supporters, until somebody finally throws the body off a cliff.

Khrushchev's de-stalinization initiative created both a public space for discussion and a new configuration of Soviet politics that outlived the Thaw: a perennial contest between 'Stalinists' and 'liberals'. Stalin's legacy 'remained the most important issue throughout the post-Stalin era', in the opinion of Soviet political insider Georgy Arbatov, with Soviet 'liberals' taking the moral high ground. This mirrored the way Soviet debate was framed in the West, as a morality play of conflict between the forces of good ('liberals') and evil ('Stalinists'). Both these terms were Western borrowings that in Soviet internal debates could only be used pejoratively, to discredit an opponent. Within the intelligentsia, attitudes to Stalinism were 'a sort of litmus test of one's attitude to life in general', one Russian told Adam Hochschild, an American journalist touring the Soviet Union in the early 1990s in search of Stalin's ghost. As construed by 'liberals', that meant a test of whether you were a decent human being or someone liable to call for your enemies to be shot. As construed by the 'Stalinists', the test was whether you were a patriot proud of your country's achievements or on the way to being a 'dissident'

'Stalinists' vs 'liberals'

(another Western term!), effectively doing the CIA's work of undermining their homeland from within.

Given the intelligentsia's claim to the moral high ground, admirers of Stalin often kept their opinion private in the late 1950s and 1960s. But that changed over time. By the 1980s, to the dismay of liberals, 'an assertive pro-Stalin lobby, proud to call itself "Stalinist"', had appeared on the political scene, although it was still a comparatively fringe group. At the height of Gorbachev's perestroika in 1989, *New Yorker* editor David Remnick still found passionate supporters of Stalin in Moscow, devoting their lives to his rehabilitation. Stalinism remained a political issue during perestroika. Licensed by Gorbachev's call for glasnost (public discussion and transparency), writers and historians leapt back into the fray, with fresh exposés of Gulag and collectivization emerging almost daily from 'the drawer', to the delight of Soviet readers. Dudintsev and Yevtushenko resurfaced to wave the old banner of the Thaw, as if the intervening thirty years had been wiped away. Gorbachev condemned Stalin-era lawlessness as 'vast and unforgivable' in an address in November 1987, noting that, whatever apologists might claim, 'Stalin knew' about it.

For Gorbachev, however, de-stalinization was a side-show; the work of publicising the evils of the Stalin period was already basically done, with only a few ends remaining for him to tidy up, such as the rehabilitation of Stalin's opponent of the early 1930s, Bukharin. What remained politically salient was whether there were achievements in the Stalin era for Soviet citizens to be proud of. But Gorbachev – unusual among Soviet leaders in identifying with the intelligentsia and looking to them for support – was not interested in going into this territory for the same reason, in reverse, as Brezhnev: the issue was too sensitive with his constituents. The perestroika debates included one notorious 'Stalinist' intervention, when the hitherto unknown Nina Andreyeva, a party member since the 1960s, published an article accusing Gorbachev of denying Soviet achievements and betraying socialism. This caused such panic among liberals in Gorbachev's team that the Politburo had to order *Pravda* to run a rebuttal – testimony to the fact that the Stalin question still mattered, even as the Soviet Union was headed for self-destruction.

Stalin in post-Soviet space

The collapse of the Soviet Union in 1991 left a Russian Federation which, under President Boris Yeltsin, went through an anarchic decade of westernization and 'wild capitalism' that offered unheard-of opportunities to some but left many others rudderless and bewildered. It was the task of Vladimir Putin, taking office as elected president of the Russian Federation in 2000 with Yeltsin's blessing, to restore order and recreate the sense of national pride and purpose shattered over the previous fifteen years. That meant, among other things, building a 'usable past' – a way of seeing Russian and Soviet history that made present-day Russians feel that they and their country were worthy of respect. In an interview in 2000, Putin described himself, not without irony, as 'a pure and utterly successful product of Soviet patriotic education', who, as a young man of working-class origins looking to make a career in the KGB, knew about Stalin's purges but had no particular interest in them or, for that matter, in Stalin. In the old Soviet fight between 'Stalinists' and 'liberals', he was an indifferent non-combatant.

Putin's take on Soviet history, like his self-irony, was unusual. The norm in Soviet debate had always been that either you liked both Lenin and Stalin (the 'Stalinist' position), or that you liked (or pretended to like) Lenin but disliked Stalin (the 'liberal' position). Putin was a man who liked Stalin but disliked Lenin. Lenin, in his view, was a nation-destroyer; his revolution had ended the Russian empire of the tsars, for which Putin had some good things to say. Stalin, on the contrary, was a nation-builder – a modernizer and industrializer who strengthened the state and made it a great power. To be sure, there were things to criticize – in 2007, President Putin would visit the Butovo execution site to unveil a monument to Stalin's innocent victims – but these issues were secondary. Putin's Stalin was, above all, the man who had led Russia/the Soviet Union to victory in the Second World War.

Lenin and Stalin according to Putin

Under Putin's rule, Soviet school history textbooks have been revised to present a more positive version of the achievements of the Stalin era. Putin took an interest in this revision, but the impulse for reassessment came as much from the

Putin and Orthodox Patriarch Alexiy II attend a memorial service at the monument to victims of Stalin's purges in Butovo, south of Moscow, on 30 October, 2007.

Russian public as from their president. In the first post-Soviet decade, a period of infatuation with the West, the Russian public was cool towards Stalin, with a poll by the independent Levada Centre finding that only 26 per cent of respondents gave a favourable assessment of the Stalin period. But by 2016, that figure had climbed to 40 per cent, and it continued to rise. As of 2019, more than half of all respondents chose respect, admiration or affection as their primary emotion about Stalin, while only 11 per cent chose enmity or fear. Moscow University's decision to install a commemorative plaque for Stalin was approved by 65 per cent of all age groups and 77 per cent of young respondents (most of whom, as other polls had established, knew little or nothing about Stalin's misdeeds). By 2022, according to the state polling agency, Stalin had joined Peter the Great and the much-venerated poet Alexander Pushkin in a troika of the most remarkable Russians of all time (using the broad term, *rossiiane,* connoting personages of the Russian empire rather than the narrower ethnic designation, *russkie*).

In the former Soviet republics, now independent states, Stalin had a varied afterlife. In Ukraine, he was the evil (Russian) dictator who had specially staged the famine of 1932–33 to kill Ukrainians, a 'genocide' which has become the founding myth of the new nation. In Georgia, on the other hand, the native son was still, to some degree, honoured. Stalin's modest birthplace in Gori remains, as in Soviet times, a tourist destination, while the large Stalin museum continues to tell the biographical story of Stalin's rise to greatness, albeit now with a carefully neutral text and the addition of a small room near the cloakroom labelled 'Russian Occupation of Georgia' which focusses on Gulag and other Soviet atrocities. With the passing of an older generation, the number of Georgians who admit to positive views of Stalin has dropped below a third; perhaps they, like Armenians in the neighbouring successor state who cited 'Stalin', along with Putin and the Kremlin, as names that came to mind when they heard the word 'Russia', are beginning to forget his original nationality. But there are still people who dream about Stalin. Such dreams of Stalin are sufficiently prevalent worldwide to have earned a dedicated website for their interpretation, but seemingly only Georgia produces a literature in which characters dream enough about Stalin to warrant a special scholarly article on the subject.

Stalin's afterlife in the republics

For some Western tourists, Stalin statues and other visual monuments of Stalinism became an object of interest – primarily ironic, but not without appreciation – in the 2010s. Stalinist chic was perhaps a passing phase. But in Western cinema, Stalin – and specifically Stalin's death – unexpectedly came into its own as a subject of comedy. It was a young Australian film-maker, Peter Duncan, who led the way in 1996 with his film *Children of the Revolution,* focussed on the last night of Stalin's life, which imagines him having sex with a young Australian Communist (played by Judy Davis) who subsequently bears his (or possibly someone else's) child. Malenkov, Khrushchev and Beria are played for laughs in the classic mode of 'the three stooges'.

In 2017, British director Armando Iannucci, whose earlier work included made-for-TV satires on US and British politics in the TV serials (*Veep* and *The Thick of It*), made a film, *The Death of Stalin*, in which black comedy blended with farce. The scenario was based on a French graphic novel by Fabien Nury and Thierry Robin, published in 2010, which picked up on the absurdist aspects of the death at the dacha as related in Khrushchev's and Svetlana's memoirs. For Nury, as for Duncan, Stalin's associates are stooges, with Beria – drawn by artist Robin in his trademark black homburg – as their malevolent leader. Stalin's son Vasily serves as the drunken comic relief and a demurely dressed Svetlana wrings her hands and weeps. Iannucci's film follows this template – but with his own twist, since his stooges are fully anglicized. Hapless British twits with a variety of class and regional accents, Iannucci's Politburo members are bullied and manipulated by the villainous Beria, who is wonderfully played by British actor Simon Russell Beale as a kind of Harley Street doctor gone rogue.

Iannucci's film was an international critical and box-office success (Barack Obama listed it as one of his favourite films in 2018). In Russia, however, it was officially seen as *lèse majesté* – 'an unfriendly act by the British intellectual class', part of a broader attempt to discredit Russia as well as Stalin. As Russian politicians vied with each other to register their protests against this 'vile, repugnant and insulting' film, 'lampooning the history of our country' and 'blackening the memory of our citizens who conquered fascism', the Ministry of Culture withdrew permission for its release in Russia. Public reaction in Russia was about equally divided between those who disapproved of the ban, approved of it, or had no opinion. But 58 per cent said they would like to watch it if they had the chance – and indeed, by January 2019, it was claimed that the film had been illegally downloaded in Russia 1.5 million times. Some former Soviet republics in Central Asia banned it as well, but it was shown in Georgia (politically split between pro-Russians and pro-Europeans) and earned some good notices. On a visit to Tbilisi in 2023, Iannucci confirmed the suspicions of the Russian censors by telling journalists that 'today's Russia is much like the one portrayed in *The Death of Stalin*' and comparing Putin to Stalin.

The masks of the dictators: Lukashenko, Putin and Stalin and on sale on the streets of St Petersburg in June 2024.

CONCLUSION

Harrison Salisbury was in Moscow when Stalin died, and (as quoted earlier) noted that it was a lucky day for Stalin's close associates. He added the rider that it was not just a lucky day for them, but for Russia and the world.

Certainly it was a lucky day for Russia (by which Salisbury meant the Soviet Union). In the first place, Stalin looked to be on the rampage again in his last years; lucky for everyone that the grim reaper interrupted him. In the second place, it was lucky for the Soviet Union (and for Stalin) that he died a natural death, and luckier still that a peaceful succession ensued. Nobody has ever suggested that Stalin deserves any credit for this, given his habit of shoring up his own position by setting his associates at odds with each other. Yet perhaps, paradoxically, some degree of credit is due. Stalin established a kind of personal dictatorship without completely abandoning Lenin's 'first among equals in the Politburo' approach to leadership. His Politburo had seemed politically insignificant to outsiders in Stalin's last years, but the men in it were used to governing and knew how to work together, with or without Stalin. Once Stalin was definitively gone, they just kept on going, and that was the basis for the successful transition.

How much trouble Stalin's death saved the world is debatable. The key issue is the Cold War, notably the degree of Stalin's responsibility for generating and continuing it. Time was when it seemed obvious in the West that the chief and perhaps sole responsibility for the Cold War lay with Stalin and the Soviet Union. Now most Western historians would put part (sometimes a large part) of the responsibility on the United States and its leaders. The idea that Stalin was planning a military onslaught on the West in the early 1950s – which would have made his death an unmixed blessing for the world – has few remaining defenders. Of course, he might have subsequently changed direction, once Soviet military strength was rebuilt and the Soviet Union had achieved nuclear parity with the United States – but so might his successors. The historical

A lucky day for the world?

Facing page: A young Communist holds a flag depicting Stalin before placing flowers on his tomb during a ceremony to mark the 71st anniversary of his death on 5 March 2024.

Stalin, as opposed to the hypothetical one, showed more inclination to talk tough to and about the West than to take it on in head-to-head conflict. The idea that Stalin's death saved the world from the Third World War is unconvincing.

Given the intense mutual suspicion between the West and Stalin, his death might conceivably have stimulated basic change in the Soviet relationship with the West – in effect an end to the Cold War. That would probably have been lucky for everyone (even though the Cold War, as a successful medium-term geopolitical alternative to hot war, looks better now than it did at the time). But it did not happen. The US, confident of its military superiority, was disinclined to détente, and Stalin's successors, though they put out some feelers after Stalin's death that were ignored, settled into a defensive posture that, over the decades, involved substantial military build-up. Stalin might have done the same. Certainly his successors were more détente-minded than Stalin had been in his last years. But Stalin, who was proud of his tactical flexibility, had been more détente-minded himself at other periods of his life.

It is on the domestic side, the impact of Stalin's death on life and politics in the Soviet Union, that the luck really comes in. It was lucky – and also remarkable – that Stalin's successors immediately embarked on an ambitious and wide-ranging programme of reform, including the abandonment of mass terror as an instrument of governance, that, over a decade, generated fundamental political, social and cultural change in Russia and the other Soviet republics. That is not to say that Stalin himself, had he lived, would have been incapable of switching course to some version of a thaw. He had done it in the mid 1930s, after the *Sturm und Drang* of collectivization and cultural revolution, and, if the decline of his last years had not signalled an irreversible decline into paranoia, might have done it again. But that is a big 'if'. In historical fact, it was Stalin's death that opened the way to the Thaw.

The collapse of the Soviet Union undid everything Stalin had worked to build – or did it? His nation-building leadership and wartime victories, hailed by Putin as the best part of the Soviet heritage, have become part of the foundation myth

Would the thaw have happened under Stalin?

96

of the post-Soviet Russian Federation. No doubt Stalin would have preferred that the country whose superpower status was gained under his watch had remained the Soviet Union. But, for the russified Georgian Stalin, becoming a latter day Peter the Great in the Russian imagination should have been a reasonable consolation prize.

Have the winds blown away the 'bunch of rubbish' dumped on Stalin's reputation, as he predicted? Not in the West, where for the foreseeable future Stalin will surely remain a bogey-man, linked with Hitler as one of the two great evildoers of the twentieth century. But in other parts of the world, particularly Russia, it's a different story. Since 2012, more than a hundred Stalin statues have gone up in Russia – most of them the result of initiatives by locals or the Communist Party rather than Putin's administration. On the seventieth anniversary of Stalin's death on 5 March 2023, hundreds came to Moscow's Red Square to pay their respects, and Russian communists requested an investigation into the possibility that, back in 1953, Western intelligence services had killed him. Stalin's memory is invoked to justify Putin's war against Ukraine, and one commentator on state media outlet, describing Stalin as 'a weapon in the battle between Russia and the West', suggested that to criticize him is 'not just anti-Soviet but is also Russo-phobic, aimed at dividing and defeating Russia'.

Bunch of rubbish?

The current pantheon of great Russian rulers runs in a line of succession from Ivan the Terrible and Peter the Great to Stalin. This is not just a whim of Putin's, but something more like an emerging popular consensus in Russia. It is hard to imagine that it will change in the foreseeable future. Status in the world is something that Russians cherish and feel they have lost. *Superpower* status in a bipolar world was a once-in-a-millennium highlight of Russian history, and Stalin was the man at the top when it happened.

ENDNOTES

Chapter 1 - STALIN

Young Stalin: Simon Sebag Montefiore, *Young Stalin* (London: Weidenfeld & Nicolson, 2007); Ronald Grigor Suny, *Stalin. Passage to Revolution* (Princeton, NJ: Princeton University Press, 2020).

(Lenin's revolution)
Lenin in power: Robert Service, *Lenin. A Biography* (Cambridge, Mass.: Harvard University Press, 2000); T. H. Rigby, *Lenin's Government. Sovnarkom 1917–1922* (Cambridge: Cambridge University Press, 1979); **formation of USSR**: E. H. Carr, *The Bolshevik Revolution, 1917–1923*, vol. 1, part 3 (Harmondsworth, Mx.: Penguin, 1966); **nationalities policy**: Ronald Grigor Suny and Terry Martin, eds., *A State of Nations: Empire and Nation-Making in the Age of Lenin and Stalin* (New York: Oxford University Press, 2001), part 1; Moshe Lewin, *Lenin's Last Struggle*, trans. A. M. Sheridan Smith (New York: Vintage Books 1970), ch. 4; **formation of Stalin's team**: Sheila Fitzpatrick, *On Stalin's Team* (Princeton, NJ: Princeton University Press, 2015), ch. 1; (Molotov quotation), Feliks Chuev, *140 besed s Molotovym* (Moscow: Terra, 1991), 260.

(Stalin's revolution)
Stalin in the 1920s: Dmitri Volkogonov, *Stalin: Triumph and Tragedy*, trans. Harold Shukman (Rocklin, CA: Prima Publishing, 1991), chs. 2-3; Stephen Kotkin, *Stalin*, vol. 1: *Paradoxes of Power* (London: Allen Lane, 2014), part 3; **succession struggle**: Robert V. Daniels, *The Conscience of the Revolution: Communist Opposition in Soviet Russia* (New York: Simon & Schuster, 1960); **'Great Break'**: Fitzpatrick, *On Stalin's Team*, ch. 2; Alec Nove, *An Economic History of the U.S.S.R.* (Harmondsworth: Penguin, 1972), chs. 6-8; **'second NEP'**: Nicolas S. Timasheff, *The Great Retreat* (New York: E. P. Dutton & Co., 1946), chs. 8-10; Sheila Fitzpatrick, *Everyday Stalinism* (New York: Oxford University Press, 1999) 90-95; **'A son does not answer for his father'**: Sheila Fitzpatrick, *Tear off the Masks! Identity and Imposture in Twentieth-Century Russia* (Princeton, NJ: Princeton University Press, 2005), 41; **Stalin and Politburo**: Fitzpatrick, *On Stalin's Team*, ch. 4; **foreign policy**: Stephen Kotkin, *Stalin*, vol. 2: *Waiting for Hitler, 1928-1941* (London: Allen Lane, 2017); Sabine Dullin, *Men of Influence. Stalin's Diplomats in Europe*, trans. Richard Veasey (Edinburgh: Edinburgh University Press, 2008); (Stalin's coaching) Fitzpatrick, On Stalin's Team; **Great Purges**; Robert Conquest, *The Great Terror: Stalin's Purge of the Thirties* (Harmondsville, Mx: Penguin, 1971); J. Arch Getty and Oleg Naumov, *The Road to Terror: Stalin and the Self-Destruction of the Bolsheviks, 1932-1939* (New Haven: Yale University Press, 1999); (draining the 'swamp'), G. A. Kumanev, *Riadom so Stalinym* (Moscow: Bylina, 1999), 78 (1991 interview with Kaganovich).

(Second World War)
Richard Overy, *Russia's War: A History of the Soviet War Effort, 1941–1945*
(New York: Penguin, 1998); John Barber and Mark Harrison, *The Soviet
Home Front 1941–1945* (London: Longman, 1991); Fitzpatrick, *On Stalin's
Team*, ch. 6.

(Leader of a superpower)
Soviet population statistics: *Naselenie Rossii v XX veke: Istoricheskie ocherki*,
vol. 2, 1940–1959, ed. Iu. A. Poliakov and V. B. Zhirmunskaia (Moscow:
ROSSPEN, 2001), 10; **Soviet geopolitics:** Stephen Lovell, *The Shadow of
War. Russia and the USSR, 1941 to the present* (Chichester: Wiley-Blackwell,
2010), 248-58; **atomic weapons:** David Holloway, *Stalin and the Bomb.
The Soviet Union and Atomic Energy, 1939–1956* (New Haven: Yale Univer-
sity Press, 1994); **Stalin cult:** Jeffrey Brooks, *Thank You, Comrade Stalin!
Soviet Public Culture from Revolution to Cold War* (Princeton, NJ: Princeton
University Pres, 2000), 94 (quotation); Victoria E. Bonnell, *Iconography of
power: Soviet political posters under Lenin and Stalin* (Berkeley: University of
California Press, 1999); Jan Plamper, *The Stalin Cult* (Stanford: Hoover In-
stitution, 2012); **70th birthday:** Nikolai Ssorin-Chaikov and Olga Sosnina,
'The Faculty of Useless Things: Gifts to Soviet Leaders', in Klaus Heller and
Jan Plamper, eds., *Personality Cults in Stalinism – Personenkulte im Stalinismus*
(Göttingen: V&R, 2004),290-1 (rug from Azerbaijan); Andrew Sobanet,
':'Homme que nous aimons le plus: French intellectuals celebrate Stalin's
70th birthday', *French Forum* 40:2/3 (2015), 54-5 (French Communists);
Jan C. Behrends, 'Exporting the Leader: the Stalin Cult in Poland and East
Germany', in Balázs Apor, *The Leader Cult in Communist dictatorships. Stalin
and the Eastern Bloc* (Houndmills, Hampshire: Palgrave Macmillan, 2004),
165-6 (Poles), 168 (East Germans); **Stalin Palace in Warsaw:** Owen Hather-
ley, *Landscapes of Communism* (np: Allen Lane, 2015), 212-19.

Chapter 2 – STALIN'S DEATH

(Postwar political tensions)
Favourable Soviet attitudes to United States: Rosemary Sullivan, *Stalin's
Daughter* (London: Fourth Estate, 2015), 127; Vladislav Zubok, *Zhiva-
go's Children* (Cambridge, MA: Harvard University Press, 2009), 39-42;
Timothy Johnston, *Being Soviet: Identity, Rumour and Everyday Life under
Stalin 1939–1953* (Oxford: Oxford University Press, 2011),167-208; **Stalin's
coaching on factional politics:** Sheila Fitzpatrick, 'Politics as Practice',
Kritika 5:1 (2004), 39-40; **anti-cosmopolitan campaign:** 'Zakrytoe pis'mo
TsK VKP(B) o dele professorov Kliuevoi i Roskina', 15 July 1947, in *Stalin i
kosmopolitizm. Dokumenty Agitpropa TsK KPSS 1945–1953* (Moscow: Materik,
2005),123-7; Fitzpatrick, *On Stalin's Team*, 191-3, 211; Simon Morrison, *Lina
& Serge. The Love and Wars of Lina Prokofiev* (New York: Houghton Mifflin
Harcourt, 2013), 245-56; **Stalin's attack on Molotov and Mikoyan:**
Fitzpatrick, *On Stalin's Team*, 211-15; Edward Radzinsky, Stalin, trans. H.T.
Willetts (New York: Doubleday, 1996), 550 ('good as dead'); Khrushchev,

Khrushchev Remembers, 309-10; A. I. Mikoian, *Tak bylo* (Moscow: Vagrius, 1990), 579-80; **antisemitic campaign and Politburo**: Fitzpatrick, *On Stalin's Team*, 200-208; Rubenstein, *Last Days*, 35-51; **Doctors' Plot**, Yoram Gorlizki and Oleg Khlevniuk, *Cold Peace*, 156-8; *Stalin i kosmopolitizm,*. 651-2 (text of *Pravda* announcement); Yakov Rapoport, *The Doctors' Plot* (London: Fourth Estate, 1967); Volkogonov, *Stalin*, 570-1 (Riumin's input); Radzinsky, *Stalin*, 553 (renewed interrogation of Molotov's wife); **scepticism in Politburo**: *Khrushchev Remembers*, 601; Gorlizki and Khlevniuk, *Cold Peace. Stalin and the Soviet ruling Circle, 1945-53* (Oxford: Oxford University Press, 2004), 161 (Bulganin); **popular reactions**: Rossiiskii gosudarstvennyi arkhiv noveishii istorii (RGANI), *fond* 5, *opis'* 15, *delo* 407; Tsentr khraneniia dokumentatsii noveishei istorii Samarskoi oblasti (TsKhDNISO), *fond* 714, *opis'* 1, *delo* 1780; **Jewish deportation rumours**: Pavel and Anatoli Sudoplatov, *Special Tasks. The Memoirs of an Unwanted Witness – a Soviet Spymaster (Boston: Little, Brown,* 1994) 308; Gorlizki and Khlevniuk, *Cold Peace*, 158-9.

(Death at the dacha)
Narratives of the death: Joshua Rubenstein, *The Last Days of Stalin* (New Haven: Yale University Press, 2016); Georges Bortoli, *Mort de Staline* (Paris: Editions Robert Laffont, 1973); *La mort de Staline* (Paris: Dargaud, 2010), graphic novel by Fabien Nury (scénario), Thierry Robin (dessin), Lorien Aureyre (couleur); *The Death of Stalin*, film directed by Armando Iannuci, co-written by David Schneider and Ian Martin (2017); **Stalin's postwar decline**: Milovan Djilas, *Conversations with Stalin*, trans. Michael B. Petrovich (Harmondsworth: Penguin, 1962), 118 (ageing); Yoram Gorlizki and Oleg Khlevniuk, *Cold Peace. Stalin and the Soviet ruling circle, 1945-1953* (Oxford: Oxford University Press, 2004), 145 (Dr Vinogradov's arrest); Nikita Khrushchev, *Khrushchev Remembers*, ed. and trans. Strobe Talbott (Boston: Little, Brown, 1970), 307 and 601 (quotations on suspicion)

Participant accounts: Khrushchev, *Khrushchev Remembers*, 315-20; Svetlana Alliluyeva, *Twenty Letters to a Friend*, trans. Priscilla Johnson (London: Hutchinson, 1967), 14-22; Sergo Beria, *Beria, My Father*, 248-9; **entourage at dacha**: Oleg Khlevniuk, *Stalin. Zhizn' odnogo vozhdia* (Moscow: AST, 2017), 61; **Rapoport's advice on doctors**: Rapoport, *Doctors' Plot*, 151-2; **Beria's explosion**: Khrushchev, *Khrushchev Remembers*, 317; **Mikoyan and Molotov summoned**: Feliks Chuev, *140 besed s Molotovym* (Moscow: Terra, 1991), 323; Mikoian, *Tak bylo*, 580; **tears of Beria's wife**: Sergo Beriia, *Moi otets Lavrentii Beriia. Syn za ottsa otvechaet...* (Moscow: Algoritm, 2013), 153 (n.b.: Russian text is not identical to English-language one); **Khrushchev weeps**: Khrushchev, *Khrushchev Remembers*, 323 (quotation); **setting up new government**: Beria, *Beria*, 248-9; Khlevniuk, *Stalin*, 422-4.
(The funeral)
Official film footage: Sergei Loznitsa, *State Funeral* (2019 documentary); **public viewing**: Harrison Salisbury, *Stalin's Russia and After* (London: MacMillan, 1955), 179 (quotation); **too many Jewish musicians?**: Rubinstein, *Last Days*, 95; **Mlynar quotation**: William Taubman, *Gorbachev. His Life*

and Times (Simon & Schuster 2017), 58; **crowd crushed ('Khodynka'):** Khlevniuk, *Stalin*, 438 (casualty figures); Yevgeny Yevtushenko, *A Precocious Autobiography*, trans. Andrew R. MacAndrew (Collins and Harvill, 1963), 89-92; Dmitrii Shepilov, *Shepilov, the Kremlin's Scholar. A Memoir of Soviet Politics under Stalin and Khrushchev*, ed. Stephen V. Bittner (New Haven: Yale University Press, 2007), 31 (quotation); **Washington's message:** text at https://www.presidency.ucsb.edu/documents/message-conveying-the-government-s-official-condolences-the-death-joseph-stalin, accessed 3 April 2024; **Pope's message:** quoted Rubinstein, *Last Days*, 122; **foreign mourning:** Rubinstein, *Last Days*, 118-123; *Nehru's speech:* text in Jawaharlal Nehru, 'Tribute to Stalin', *Labour Monthly* XXXV:4 (April 1953). https://www.marxists.org/subject/stalinism/1953/stalin.htm, accessed 30 March 2024.

Chapter 3 – POPULAR REACTIONS

Tears: Irina Paperno, *Stories of the Soviet Experience: Memoirs, Diaries, Dreams* (Ithaca, NY: Cornell University Press, 2009), 27; Yevtushenko, *Precocious Autobiography*, 89; Denis Kozlov, *Readers of Novy Mir* (Cambridge, MA: Harvard UP, 2013, 142-3; Morrison, *Lina & Serge*, 170; **shock:** Irina Paperno, 'Intimacy and Power: Soviet Memoirists Remember Stalin', in Heller and Plamper, *Personality Cults*, 345; Yevtushenko, *Precocious Autobiography*, 28; Paperno, *Stories* (Orlova quotation), 28; Ilya Ehrenburg, *The Post-War Years 1945–1954*, vol, VI of *Men, Years, Life*, trans. Tatiana Shebunina (London: Macgibbon & Kees, 1966), 302; Beria, *Beria*, 249; Salisbury, *Stalin's Russia*, 168; **Master dead:** Abram Tertz (Andrei Sinyavsky), *The Trial Begins. On Socialist Realism*, trans Max Hayward (Berkeley: University of California Press, 1960.

(Reactions and reassessments)
'leathery cacti': Edward Crankshaw, *Khrushchev's Russia* (Harmondsworth, Mx: Penguin, 1959), 38; **Beria and Mikoyan shock their sons:** Beria, *Beria*, 238; Stepan A. Mikoian, *Vospominaniia voennogo letchika-ispytatelia* (Moscow: Tekhnika molodezhi, 2002), 197;
'Luckiest thing': Salisbury, *Stalin's Russia*, 161; **Beria's comment to Molotov:** Chuev, *140 besed*, 327-8; **murder by Beria 'impossible':** Sudoplatov, *Special Tasks*, 333; **Simonov comment:** quoted Radzinsky, *Stalin*, 566; **rumours of murder:** letters to the Party Central Committee, reported 19 March 1953, RGANI, *fond* 5, *opis'* 15, *delo* 407; **suggestions for memorialization:** Iurii Aksiutin, *Khrushchevskaia "ottepel" i obshchestvennye nastroeniia v SSSR v 1953-1954 gg.* (Moscow: ROSSPEN, 2004), 19; **suggestions on succession:** Rossiiskii gosudarstvennyi arkhiv sotsial'no-politicheskoi istorii (RGASPI), *fond* 82, *opis'* 2, *delo* 1466; ll. 26, 36, 44-50, 58 (files of letters to Molotov); Shepilov, *Kremlin's Scholar*, 256; **mocking rumours:** Vladimir A. Kozlov, Sheila Fitzpatrick, and Sergei V. Mironenko, eds., *Sedition. Everyday Resistance in the Soviet Union under Khrushchev and Brezhnev* ((New Haven: Yale University Press, 2011), 68-78.

(New directions)
Immediate radical policy changes: Fitzpatrick, *On Stalin's Team*, 227-8; **Beria quotation**: Beria, *Beria*, 249-50; **Beria on downsizing Gulag**: Golfo Alexopoulos, *Illness and Inhumanity in Stalin's Gulag* (New Haven: Yale University Press, 2017), 134; **Gulag amnesty**: Amy Knight, *Beria. Stalin's First Lieutenant* (Princeton NJ: Princeton University Press, 1993), 185; **release of doctors**: text in *Stalin i kosmopolitizm*, 654, note 2; **reversal of russification**: Gerhard Simon, *Nationalism and Policy towards the Nationalities in the Soviet Union*, trans. Karen Forster and Oswald Forster (Boulder: Westview, 1991), 228 (quotation); Fitzpatrick, *On Stalin's Team*, 230-31; **economic reforms**: Roger W. Opdahl, 'Soviet Agriculture since 1953', *Political Science Quarterly* 75:1 (1960), 57; Nove, *Economic History*, 324-6; **'conflictlessness'**: Maz Hayward and Leopold Labedz, eds., *Literature and Revolution in Soviet Russia, 1917-1962* (London Oxford University Press, 1963), 117-8, 158-9; **Soviet film output**: Peter Kenez, *Cinema and Soviet Society* (London: I. B. Tauris, 2001), 187-8; **cultural Thaw**: Crankshaw, *Khrushchev's Russia*, 99 (quotation), 102-9, 110 (quotation); **Khrushchev's fears**: Nikita Khrushchev, *Khrushchev Remembers. The Last Testament* (Boston: Little, Brown, 1974), 78-9; **negative reactions to doctors' release**: RGANI, *fond* 5, *opis'* 30, *delo* 5, ll. 9, 23, 43; RGASPI, *fond* 82, *opis'* 2, *delo* 1466, l. 58; **to Gulag amnesty**: Robert Hornsby, *The Soviet Sixties* (New Haven: Yale University Press, 2023), 30 (first two quotations); Miriam Dobson, ''Show the Bandit-Enemies No Mercy': Amnesty, Criminality and Public Response in 1953', Polly Jones, ed., *Dilemmas of De-Stalinization* (London: Routledge, 2006), 30-31 (third and fourth quotations).

(Ousting of Beria)
Khrushchev's ambush: Khrushchev, *Khrushchev Remembers*, 322-41; Mikoian, *Tak eto bylo*, 586-7; Chuev, *140 besed s Molotovym*, 343-6; **indictment of Beria**: text (from *Pravda* 17 December 1953) in *Politbiuro i delo Beriia. Sbornik dokumentov*, ed. O. B. Mozokhina (Moscow: Kuchkovo pole, 2012), 549-552; **rumours about Beria's downfall**: RGANI, *fond* 5, *opis'* 30, *delo* 4, l. 21 and *opis'* 15, *delo* 407, ll. 114-17; 'Informatsiia ob otklikakh trudiashchikhsia ot 10 iiulia 1953 g. na Postanovlenie Plenuma TsK KPSS o prestupnykh antipartiinykh i antigosudarstvennykh deistviiakh Beriia', in *Politbiuro i delo Beriia*,1002-4.

Chapter 4 - REACTIONS ABROAD

Eisenhower quotation: Emmet John Hughes, *The Ordeal of Power. A Political Memoir of the Eisenhower Years* (New York: Atheneum, 1963), 101.

(US and Soviet stereotypes)
NSC-68: Stephen Kinzer, *The Brothers. John Foster Dulles, Allen Dulles, and their Secret World War* (New York: St Martins Griffin, 2013), 96-7 (quotations); **totalitarianism**: David C. Engerman, *Know your Enemy. The Rise*

and Fall of America's Soviet Experts), New York: Oxford University Press, 2009), 206 (Truman Doctrine quotation); Carl J. Friedrich, *Totalitarianism. Proceedings of a conference held at the American Academy of Arts and Sciences, March 1953* (Cambridge, MA: Harvard University Press, 1954); Merle Fainsod, *How Russia is Ruled* (Cambridge, MA: Harvard University Press, 1953), 500 (quotation); **Novikov telegram:** text in *Origins of the Cold War. The Novikov, Kennan, and Roberts "Long Telegrams" of 1946,* ed. Kenneth M. Jensen (Washington, DC: United States Institute of Peace, 1991), 3-16; **Stalin on peace:** interviews with Harold Stassen (9 April 1947), UN General Secretary Trygve Lih (15 May 1950), *Pravda* correspondent (17 February 1951) and US correspondent James Reston (21 December 1952) in I. V. Stalin, *Sochineniia,* vol. 16 (Moscow: ITRK, 2011), part 1, 490; part 2, 317, 318, 565; **Soviet diplomatic style:** ('malevolent' Molotov) Alan Bullock, *Ernest Bevin, Foreign Secretary, 1945-1951* (Oxford: Oxford University Press, 1983), 199; (Molotov and Dulles) Anatoly Dobrynin, *In Confidence. Moscow's Ambassador to America's Six Cold War Presidents (1962-1986)* (New York: Random House, 1995), 26 (quotation); (Dulles on Vyshinsky) Kinzer, *Brothers,* 85.

(Intelligence wars)
'Fifth column' fears: Vladimir O. Pechatnov, 'The Soviet Union and the World', in *The Cambridge History of the Cold War*, vol. 1, ed. Melvyn P. Leffler and Odd Arne Westad (Cambridge: Cambridge University Press, 2010), 107; **Western intelligence failure:** Stephen Dorril, *MI6, Fifty Years of Special Operations* (London: Fourth Estate, 2000), 66 (British ignorance quotation); Harry Rositzke, *The CIA's Special Operations: Espionage, counterespionage and Covert Action* (New York: Readers' Digest, 1977), 20 (US files and Soviet spies quotations), 16 (intelligence failure quotation); **dismissal of Soviet 'peace talk':** Dorril, *MI6,* 500 (quotations).

(Eisenhower and John Foster Dulles)
Attitudes towards communism: Kinzer, *Brothers,* 109 ('lightness and dark'), 84 ('challenge to civilization'), 108 ('massive retaliation'); **response to Stalin's death:** Kinzer, *Brothers,* 133 (Mossadeq); Hughes, *Ordeal,* 102 ('salutary silence'); Gregory Mitrovich, *Undermining the Kremlin. America's Strategy to Subvert the Soviet Bloc, 1947-1950* (London and Ithaca: Cornell University Press, 2000), 130 ('family funeral'), 106 ('winning World War III'); **'Chance for Peace':** Dwight D. Eisenhower, *The White House Years,* vol. 1: *Mandate for Change* (London: Heinemann, 1963), 144-5; Dwight Eisenhower, Address 'The Chance for Peace' delivered before the American Society of Newspaper Editors, https://www.presidency.ucsb.edu/documents/address-the-chance-for-peace-delivered-before-the-american-society-newspaper-editors, accessed 5 May 2024 (quotations); **Churchill's support:** Dorril, *MI6,* 500-05; **Eisenhower's failure to follow up:** Hughes, *Ordeal,* 118 (playing golf); **US experts' advice:** Mitrovich, *Undermining,* 135, 120 ('Soviet vulnerabilities' report); Eisenhower, *White House Years* I, 149 ('cautious game'); **psychological warfare:** Rositzke, *CIA's*

Special Operations, 149-50; Mitrovich, *Undermining*, 81 and 78; **'liberation'** **strategy**: Kinzer, *Brothers*, 166-7 (Dulles quotation); https://nsarchive2. gwu.edu/NSAEBB/NSAEBB50/doc74.pdf, accessed 4 May 2024 (text of NSC 158); **use of Soviet 'displaced persons'**: Benjamin Tromly, *Cold War Exiles and the CIA* (Oxford: Oxford University Press, 2019), part 3; Rositzke, *CIA's Special Operations*, 22, 26, 38; **Soviet hesitancy**: Dobrynin, *In Confidence*, 26; Georgi Arbatov, *The System. An Insider's Life in Soviet Politics* (New York: Random House, 1993), 41.

Chapter 5 – STALIN'S GHOST

'bunch of rubbish' quotation: Chuev, *140 besed*, 327; **Yugoslavs**: Khrushchev, *Khrushchev Remembers. The Glasnost Tapes* (Boston: Little, Brown & Co, 1990), 103-4; **returnees from Gulag**: Stephen F. Cohen, *The Victims Return* (London: I. B. Tauris, 2011), esp. 88-90.

(Denunciation of Stalin cult, 1956)
Discussion of Pospelov report: quotations from *Prezidium TsK KPSS 1954-1964*, vol. 1. *Chernovye protokol'nye zapisi zasedanii. Stenogrammy*, ed. A. A. Fursenko (Moscow: ROSSPEN, 2003), 99-103 (note that I continue to use the term 'Politburo' for the party's top organ, although from 1952 to 1966 it was formally called 'the Presidium'); **'Secret Speech'**: 'Khrushchev's Secret Speech', Appendix 4 in Khrushchev, *Khrushchev Remembers*, esp. 596-7, 600-01, 610-11; **Resolution**: 'On the Cult of Personality and its Consequences', 25 February 1956, *XX s'ezd Kommunisticheskoi Partii Sovetskogo Soiuza. Stenograficheskii otchet*, part 2 (Moscow: Gos. Izdat.polit.lit., 1956), 498; **Svetlana weeps**: Sullivan, *Stalin's Daughter*, 216; **reactions**: Taubman, *Gorbachev*, 97 (Stavropol); O. Leibovich et al, eds., *1956: Nezamechennyi termidor. Ocherki provintsial'nogo byta* (Perm: Permskii gosudartvewnnyii. institute iskusstva i kul'tury, 2012), 58 (Molotovo); Stephen V. Bittner, *The Many Lives of Khrushchev's Thaw* (Ithaca, NY: Cornell University Press, 2008), 54-65 (Gnesin School); **Georgians offended**: Khrushchev, *Khrushchev Remembers*, appendix 4, 599; Timothy K. Blauvelt and Jeremy Smith, eds., *Georgia after Stalin* (London: Routledge, 2016); Timothy Blauvelt, 'Status Shift and Ethnic Mobilization in the March 1956 Events in Georgia', *Europe-Asia Studies* 61:4 (2009), 651-668.

(Cracks in the collective leadership)
Kaganovich on Khrushchev: Lazar Kaganovich, *Pamiatnye zapiski* (Moscow: Vagrius, 1997), 510; **'anti-party group' ousted**: *Molotov, Malenkov, Kaganovich 1957: Dokumenty* (Moscow: Mezhdunarodnyi fond 'Demokratiia', 1998), 118 (Molotov), 119 (Khrushchev), 398 (Kaganovich); Hornsby, *Soviet Sixties*, 127-8; **Twenty-Second Party Congress 1961**: *XII s'ezd KPSS: stenograficheskii otchet* (Moscow, 1962), vol 3, 119-21 (Lazurkina); Taubman, *Khrushchev*, 514 ('swamp creatures'); **removal of Stalin's body**: Taubman, *Khrushchev*, 514-15; **statues removed**: Taubman, *Gorbachev*, 98; **renaming**: Plamper, *Stalin Cult*, 258 n.14; **Yevtushenko poem** (Russian text, my trans-

lation): Evgenii Evtushenko, 'Nasledniki Stalina': https://www.culture.ru/poems/26385/nasledniki-stalina, accessed 12 May 2024.

('Stalinists' and 'liberals')
Soviet attitudes: Hedrick Smith, *The Russians* (New York: Ballantine Books, 1976), 325, 327 (quotations); **Brezhnev's attitude**: Susanne Schattenberg, *Brezhnev. The Making of a Statesman*, trans John Heath (London: I. B. Tauris, 2022), 247-8; **petition**: Hornsby, *Soviet Sixties*, 327-8; **Tvardovsky diary**: Aleksandr Tvardovskii, *Novomirskii dnevnik*, vol. 2 (Moscow: Prozaik, 2009), 18, 44, 46 (diary entries for 13 March and 2 and 4 July, 1967); **Kremlin Wall graves**: https://en.wikipedia.org/wiki/Kremlin_Wall_Necropolis"Site , accessed 8 May 2024; **dreams of Stalin**: Paperno, *Stories*, 43, 161-208; **Solzhenitsyn's Stalin**: Alexander Solzhenitsyn, *The First Circle* (London: Collins Harvill, 1988), trans. Max Hayward, Manya Harari and Michael Glenny, 90-120 (the novel was written between 1955 and 1964); **dissident celebrations**: Benjamin Nathans, *To the Success of our Hopeless Cause* (Princeton, NJ: Princeton University Press, 2024), 543; **Stalinism as political issue**: Arbatov, *System*, 45; **'truth about ourselves'**: Stephen F. Cohen, 'The Stalin Question since Stalin', in Stephen F. Cohen, ed., *An End to Silence. Uncensored Opinion in the Soviet Union from Roy Medvedev's Underground Magazine Political Diary* (New York: Norton, 1982), 29 (1962 quotation); Adam Hochschild, *Unquiet Ghost. Russians Remember Stalin* (New York: Viking, 1994), 116; **'pro-Stalin lobby'**: Cohen, 'Stalin Question', 42-3; **Stalin rehabilitators**: David Remnick, 'In the glasnost' era, a cadre of loyalists stuck in time', *Washington Post*, 15 November 1989; **Gorbachev address**: Taubman. *Gorbachev*, 321; **Andreyeva's article**: Taubman, *Gorbachev*, 345-51.

(Stalin in post-Soviet space)
Putin: Putin speech of 16 January 2016 in "Zasedanie mezhregional'nogo foruma ONF, 'kremlin.ru/events/president/transcripts/51206, accessed 4 June 2024; Natalia Gevorkyan et al, *First Person: an astonishingly frank self-portrait by Russia's President Vladimir Putin* (New York: Public Affairs, 2000); Dina Khapaeva, *Putin's Dark Ages: Political Neomedievalism and Re-Stalinization in Russia* (London: Routledge, 2023), 159-71; **Volgograd/Stalingrad**: Eva Hartog, 'Russia invades Ukraine: One year on', 21 Feb 2023: https://www.politico.eu/article/siege-stalingrad-battle-bucha-vladimir-putin-russia-war-against-west/, accessed 8 May 2024; **opinion polls**: http://www.levada.ru/2016/03/01/praviteli-v-otechestvennoj-istorii/; https://www.levada.ru/en/2019/19/dynamic-of-stalin-s-perception; https://wciom.com/press-release/memory-of-stalin-pro-et-contra,; https://www.themoscowtimes.com/2018/10/05/half-russian-youth-say-theyre-unaware-of-stalinist-repressions-poll-a63104; https://www.miloserdie.ru/article/populyarnost-stalina-rastet-chto-s-nami-ne-tak/, all accessed 8 April 2024; **Ukrainian view**: Anne Applebaum, *Red Famine. Stalin's War on Ukraine* (np: Allen Lane, 2017), 347-61; https://www.atlanticcouncil.org/blogs/ukrainealert/many-ukrainians-see-putins-invasion-as-a-con-

tinuation-of-stalins-genocide/, accessed 11 May 2024; 347-61; **Georgian and Armenian views**: information based on recent Caucasus Research Research Centers surveys from Sona Balasanyan (dir. CRRC, Armenia) and Koba Turmanidze (dir. CRRC, Georgia), Tbilisi, Monterey Summer Symposium on Russia, Yerevan, 3 July 2024 and Tbilisi, 13 July 2024; **Russian reactions to Iannucci**: Shaun Walker, 'In Russia, nobody's laughing at Iannucci's *The Death of Stalin*', *Guardian*, 14 Oct 2017; Marc Bennetts, 'Russia pulls "despicable" *Death of Stalin* from cinemas', *Guardian*, 24 January 2018; Alex Ritman, 'Armando Iannucci on "Death of Stalin" Success, Censorship and why he ditched his Trump film idea', *Hollywood Reporter*, 11 January 2019; **Iannucci in Georgia**: RFE/RFL Georgian Service and Vazha Tavberidze, '"Veep" director Iannucci says Putin may be left only with "shadow"', https://www.rferl.org/a/veep-director-iannucci-putin-ukraine-russia-shadow-/32459290.html, accessed 3 June 2024.

CONCLUSION

(Stalin's reputation in Putin's Russia)
New Stalin statues: Jade McGlynn, 'What the West gets wrong on Stalin and Putin', CNN Opinion, 20 January 2024, https://edition.cnn.com/2024/01/20/opinions/new-stalin-centers-russia-putin-mcglynn/index.html, accessed 29 July 2024; **70th anniversary of Stalin's death:** 'Putin's Russia summons Stalin from the grave as wartime ally', https://www.politico.eu/article/vladimir-putin-russia-summon-joseph-stalin-grave-wartime-ally/#:~:text=Seventy%20years%20after%20his%20death,who%20want%20to%20stifle%20dissent.&text=MOSCOW%20%E2%80%94%20As%20Russia%20enters%20the,renewed%20alignment%20with%20the%20Kremlin;:https://www.reuters.com/world/russia-communist-wing-asks-probe-into-wests-possible-involvement-stalins-death-2024-03-05/, accessed 29 July 2024.

IMAGE CREDITS TK

ACKNOWLEDGEMENTS

I thank Ben Yarde-Buller of Old Street Publishing for coming up with the idea of this book and persuading me to write it, and my ACU colleague Lisa O'Connell and Black, Inc publisher Chris Feik for acting as sounding boards.

Numerous conversations with admirers of Iannucci's *The Death of Stalin* made me realise that his film has embedded unforgettable images and a particular view of the event in the minds of anglophone readers. So I have played off his film (which I loved) in my account.

I also consulted many friends on the identification of Beria's black hat as a homburg. This convinced me that even people with long memories have forgotten anything they ever knew about respectable men's hattery in the 1950s.

G R E A T  E V E N T S

Great Events are short, lively books of narrative history, written by experts but aimed squarely at the general reader, about the most dramatic and consequential events of the past 150 years. The series launches in early 2025 with *The Death of Stalin* by Sheila Fitzpatrick and *Bombard the Headquarters!* by Linda Jaivin. In time, we hope *Great Events* will offer an indispensable 'map of the territory', helping readers to follow their interests and chart their own course through the past.

For more information please write to the publisher at
info@oldstreetpublishing.co.uk